THE COMPLETE GUIDE TO REAL ESTATE INVESTMENT IN ARGENTINA
(Third Edition)

Simon A. Fawkes

Published by
Lansdowne Press

Published by Lansdowne Press 2011

Copyright © Simon A. Fawkes 2011

Simon A. Fawkes has asserted his right under the Copyright, Designs and Patents Act, 1998 to be identified as the author of this work

This book is sold subject to the condition that it shall not by way of trade or otherwise be lent, resold, hired out, or otherwise circulated without the publisher's prior consent in any form of binding or cover other than that which it is published and without a similar condition including this condition being imposed upon the subsequent purchaser

First published in 2006 by
Lansdowne Press in partnership with Lulu Inc.

Second Edition published 2008

www.simon-a-fawkes.info

ISBN 978-1-257-17637-3

All rights reserved. No part of this publication may be reproduced, stored on a retrieval system, or transmitted in any form or by any means, without prior permission of the publishers.

Printed in the EU and the US - see back page for details

The Provinces of Argentina (image courtesy of Wikipedia)

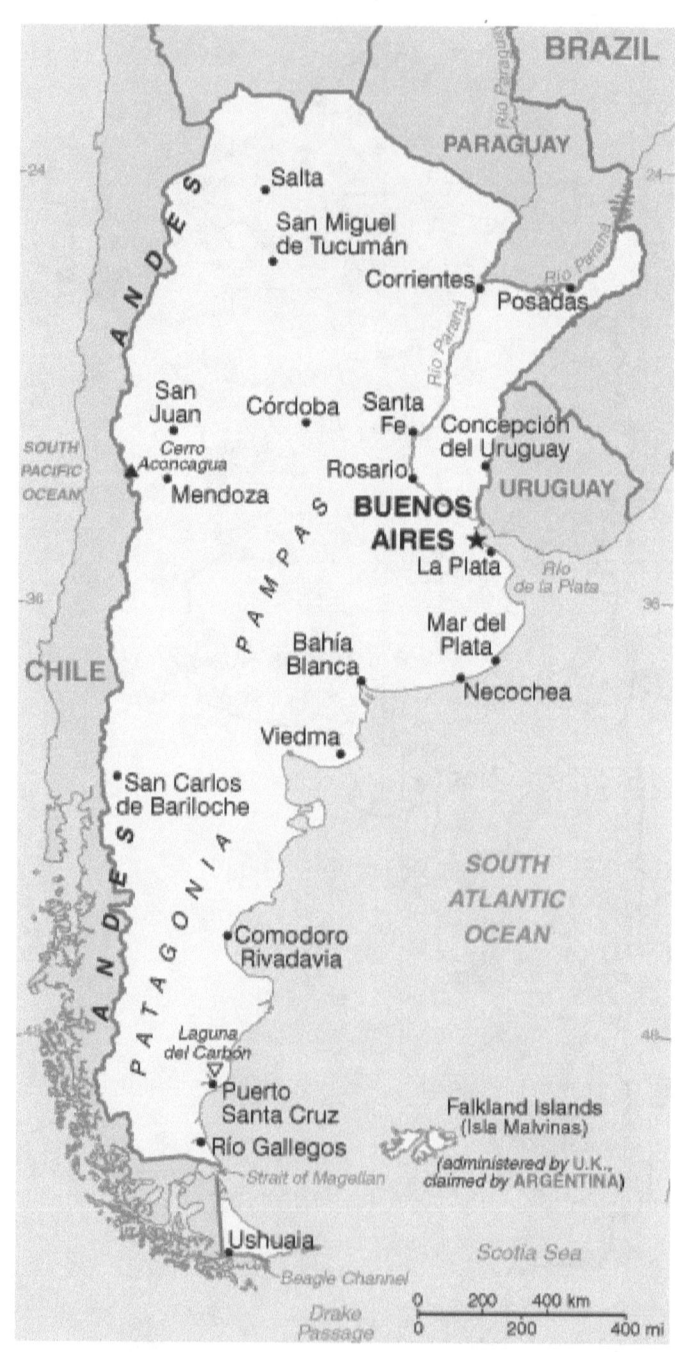

Major Cities In Argentina (image courtesy of Wikipedia)

Contents

1. About This Book 6
2. Background To The Book 8
3. Legal Note 11
4. Language & Terminology 12
5. Why Invest In Real Estate In Argentina? 13
6. How Safe Is Argentina? 17
7. Information About Argentina 19
8. Real Estate In The Capital - An Overview 24
9. Buying a Home versus Buying For Investment 29
10. Buying as a Private Individual versus Buying As a Corporation 34
11. Using a Property Investment Consultant versus Going It Alone 41
12. The Return on Investment (ROI) 46
13. Choosing Areas of Buenos Aires To Invest In 51
14. Finding Suitable Property For Sale 63
15. Choosing A Realtor *(inmobiliaria)* 72
16. The Difference Between Realtors & Property Investment Consultants 74
17. Viewing Properties - Factors To Consider 76
18. The Property Specification Sheet 88
19. How Many Times To See a Place Before Making An Offer 91
20. Making An Offer 92
21. Building Surveys 98
22. Escribanos - What They Do And How To Choose One 99
23. What Happens Once The Offer Is Agreed: Boletos, Senas and Escrituras 103
24. Things To Organize Before The Escritura 110
25. Post-purchase Costs (Running Expenses) 126
26. Opening A Bank Account 135
27. Renting Out Property 137
28. Choosing a Rental Agent *(agente de alquiler)* 142
29. Taxation Issues 146
30. Refurbishing Real Estate 149
31. Furnishing Property 157
32. Sample ROI calculation 163
33. Investing In Real Estate Outside Of Buenos Aires 166
34. Multiple Property Ownership 168
35. Selling Real Estate 169
36. Residency And Citizenship 174
37. Death And Inheritance *(sucesion)* 178
38. Glossary 180
39. Supplementary Appendix Information 187

The Complete Guide To Real Estate Investment In Argentina

1. About This Book

This book gives you all the hard facts you need to know about property investment in Argentina. It assumes you are not Argentinean and know nothing about Argentina with respect to its local laws, customs, processes, taxes, banking and cultural matters related to real estate ownership and connected issues. It contains detailed information on a complete range of topics including everything you need to know about buying, selling, owning and renting property in Argentina, and the common pitfalls and scams to avoid.

As well as the actual property acquisition process, the book also covers the numerous after-care aspects which often cause a problem for foreigners. Subjects include post-purchase costs, opening a bank account, refurbishing and furnishing property, residency and inheritance issues, plus many others.

The book tells you all you need to know about renting out your newly-acquired property as an investment. The merits of short-term versus long-term rentals are covered, along with selecting and dealing with agents and tenants and the tax regime.

In short, this book gives you all the hard facts you need to know about the above topics and more - i.e. *what* you need to know. To complement this book, the author also sells a supplementary appendix that can be bought from www.simon-a-fawkes.info. The supplementary appendix is updated regularly and contains specific information about recommended businesses and individuals - e.g. consultants, realtors, lawyers and rental agents etc. that are known to be trustworthy and reliable - in short the very people you should

1. About This Book

be doing business with so that you can invest in Argentinean real estate with complete confidence that you are not being exploited or ripped off. Further details can be found in the *Supplementary Appendix Information* chapter. Taken together, the book and the supplementary appendix provide a complete guide not just to *what* you need to know, but also crucially to *who* you need to know to successfully invest in Argentinean real estate.

The process of buying property is similar in all of Argentina's 23 provinces. As 98% of foreign investors buy in Buenos Aires, this book primarily focuses on real estate investment in the capital. In some provinces there may be minor differences and different local taxes may apply. More information can be found in the *Investing Outside Of Buenos Aires* chapter.

Likewise, as the vast majority of foreign buyers will buy an apartment in a block as opposed to a house, the text will for the most part assume that this is the case. The process for buying a house is the same, although some factors won't be relevant and can be ignored. These should be obvious.

This third edition of the guide has been updated and revised to reflect relevant changes since the second edition was published, and contains the latest available figures and prices.

2. Background To The Book

In 2000 I was working in Buenos Aires for a global financial corporation. The company provided me with a nice apartment in the center of Buenos Aires. Over time I made many local friends and realized I would like to make a base here. So I decided I would buy my own apartment. It would be easy, so I thought...but I couldn't have been more wrong.

In one sense buying in Argentina is pretty much the same as buying anywhere else in the world. You view properties, decide on one you like, make an offer, probably haggle a little over the cost, then once the price is agreed you instruct a property lawyer to complete the formalities and the funds are transferred. The difference is that in Argentina there are many traps for the unwary to fall into, including fraudsters that will try to rip you off or scam you at every opportunity. These include many apparently reputable firms, such as dodgy realtors, lawyers charging phantom property taxes, real estate consultants who charge exorbitant fees but deliver little or nothing, corrupt sellers insisting that the purchase price is officially recorded at a lower figure so they can fiddle their taxes, to list just a few.

Nowhere was there an official guide to the buying process, nor could I find a complete source of information. I had to rely on what I was told by the so-call professionals. At first I took what people said at face value, although alarm bells began to ring when different people gave me different, often conflicting, advice. They couldn't all be right.

2. Background To The Book

My friends in Buenos Aires were concerned too, and some told me that some of the things I had been told were just plain wrong. Even friends that had gone through the process themselves and had bought their own property were in disagreement about certain points. This was truly worrying.

Eventually, with the help of my friends, and after a lot of my own patient research and enquiries, I found a realtor (estate agent) I was comfortable using. With their help I found a really nice apartment in the Palermo district and made an offer on it. After a bit of negotiation with the owner, the offer was accepted. Again with the help of my friends, I found a good lawyer that spoke English that I felt I could trust.

That was the easy bit. One of the most difficult aspects of the whole buying process was getting the purchase cash into the country and into the hands of the seller. Yes, cash. Almost all property transactions in Argentina are in cash - the people here do not trust the banking system (more on this in later chapters). Also it makes false reporting of the sale price much easier. Again, after a lot of research, I found a cheap, easy and safe way to bring funds into the country.

Eventually I took possession of my treasured apartment. I had wasted a huge amount of my time tying to get to grips with the property purchase process and understand the details of its complexities and subtleties, and the traps for the unwary and how ultimately they could have cost me a lot more money if I had fallen into them. I had been through a huge learning curve but ultimately I was pleased with my apartment. No pain, no gain, as they say.

The Complete Guide To Real Estate Investment In Argentina

On the back of this experience (well actually it's a bit more complicated than that, but I won't bore you with the details), friends and their acquaintances began to come to me for advice about buying property, and through getting involved with these people and their purchases my knowledge of the real estate market in Buenos Aires grew, allowing me to become the expert I am on it today. Over the years I've been involved in various aspects of dozens of apartment purchases, and have provided my services to many professional investors who are interested in both the capital appreciation potential and the income possibilities from renting out their property.

This book isn't just about my knowledge of buying property. It also covers issues beyond the purchase which many real estate consultants know little about, such as dealing with refurbishment and how to go about renting your property, both areas with which I have had extensive experience through helping my clients.

Although my experience has been mainly dealing with property in Buenos Aires, unless otherwise stated the principals and laws apply just as equally to real estate in the rest of Argentina.

This book (the *what* aspect), and its supplementary appendix that includes details of trusted businesses and individual contacts (the *who* aspect), are the result of my many years experience in this field.

3. Legal Note

The information in this book is provided in good faith, however neither the author nor the publisher will accept any liability for any errors or bad investment decisions made as a result of the material it contains.

4. Language & Terminology

The official language in Argentina is Spanish and many of the things described in this book have Spanish names. For example, realtors (estate agents) are known as *inmobiliaria*. To aid readability I will use the corresponding English terms in the text as most readers will be familiar with these. The first time a term is used the Spanish name will be given alongside in italics. A full list can be found in the glossary.

The above example illustrates another language problem - usage differences between British English and American English. As this book is aimed more at the American market I have used the American terminology - e.g. realtor rather than estate agent. Again, a list of the most common differences that relate to the subject matter can be found in the glossary.

As I have a British background it's possible that I've used a few British words that won't be familiar to some American readers. If any have slipped through the net, I apologize.

For simplicity all prices are given in US dollars. Prices are indicative and are provided as a rough guide only. Annual inflation in 2011 is officially running at around 10% (and unofficially closer to 25%), so in all probability prices will have increased and be higher than those stated.

5. Why Invest In Real Estate In Argentina?

In a nutshell, because there are some fantastic investment opportunities. Property in prime locations, notably central Buenos Aires, can cost as little as only a tenth of what comparable properties would sell for in the United States or Europe. Long term, there are great capital gains opportunities, and in the shorter term rental yields upwards of 8% can be achieved. Oh, and it's a great place to live or visit.

Property is cheap for those armed with foreign currency. Values are pegged to the US dollar and the real estate sector accounted for sixty per cent of all investment in Argentina in 2006, in which year, by some estimates, a third to a half of luxury apartment purchases in Buenos Aires were by foreigners - unsurprising when you consider what a relatively small sum could buy. Although the market has remained flat from 2008 due to the global recession, as of 2011 one-bed apartments can still cost less than US$80,000, and you could pick up a stylish two-bed place from upwards of US$110,000.

Ninety-nine point nine percent of property transactions in Argentina are in cash (US dollars). Yes, cash. Because people pay in cash it creates a stable market, more so than in countries like the UK and US where most property is heavily leveraged (mortgaged) and prices are therefore more subject to interest rate and economic changes.

In 2001 - 2002 Argentina's economy suffered a major collapse. The Argentinean peso had been kept artificially high by being officially pegged at one-to-one with the US dollar. Over time this built up into an untenable situation that lead to the peso-dollar tie being abandoned. The value of the peso, now a free-floating currency, was determined by the global currency markets.

The breaking of the peso-dollar tie caused the peso to devalue 70% against the dollar in late 2002. It went from 1:1 to over 3:1 almost overnight. This made previously-attractive dollar mortgages cripplingly expensive. Saddled with spiralling personal debts and unmanageable dollar mortgages many home owners were desperate to sell their property to salvage something. With many sellers and few buyers, the property market collapsed.

During this time many people lost the majority of their savings and their pensions. Draconian laws were put in place to prevent the banking system from collapsing. Because of this most Argentineans lost all trust in the banks, which is one of the reasons why virtually all property transactions are in cash today.

Following the crash a major economic recovery began and now the economy is thriving again, thanks to a revival in exports (now cheap for foreign buyers) and domestic demand. At the end of 2003 residential property had recovered to about 70% of its pre-crash value, and by the start of 2007 many areas had recovered to their pre-crash level. Property transactions, including new-build completions, reached a new record in late 2006. There was an average 18% appreciation in the year 2007/2008.

One key reason why confidence returned to the market so quickly is that many Argentineans did not (and still don't) trust the banks and regard land and property as a more secure investment.

5. Why Invest in Real Estate In Argentina?

Following the crash it was difficult for most people to get mortgages, although attempts are being made to make it easier as the government is now taking steps to encourage people to do so. However, interest rates of 14% and more make them largely unaffordable for the local population, and still in 2011 there are virtually no mortgage-funded purchases. Easy credit and excessive leverage have not made up the foundations of the Argentinean real estate boom. In other words, it's almost bubble-proof - at least for the foreseeable future.

Argentina's real estate market has a long way to go and will probably never command prices on par with Europe or the States, but if the discount goes from one-tenth the price to two-tenths the price, real estate prices will have doubled. That's a small step for a market that is only beginning to use housing loans.

Foreign money flowing into Buenos Aires' housing market helped property values rebound, particularly at the top-end of the market. Even though real estate prices soared up to 2008 they still look surprisingly cheap to outsiders.

In 2008 many forecasters were predicting that prices would at least double within six years. However, the global recession kicked in, but unlike in many countries where property markets collapsed, in Argentina the market held firm with prices remaining steady with reports of only a 2 or 3% variation (both up and down). This is primarily due to the fact that property prices are based on hard cash value and not easy credit or leverage as was the case elsewhere. There was no property market crash in Argentina,

The Complete Guide To Real Estate Investment In Argentina

although the overall volume of transactions was down significantly and remains so as of early 2011.

The general consensus in early 2011 is that prices are likely to remain flat, or only rise slightly whilst the world's economy remains in recession. Once things are back to normal (if they ever do get back) then it's widely expected that prices will continue to rise as previously predicted; in other words the global recession will have stalled price growth for a few years, but over the long term the previous upwards trend is likely to continue.

Although the general inflation rate is high in Argentina, and has been for years, this hasn't really impacted on real estate prices. This is because prices are stated in US$, which are somewhat at arms length from the high inflation of the Argentine peso.

Another factor which bodes well for the property market is that buying property in Argentina is straightforward (although there are many scams and rip-offs to catch the unwary). Foreign investors may buy without permission in most municipalities, and buying as a private investor there is no capital gains tax when you come to sell.

For many buyers Buenos Aires is less about the deal and more about the lifestyle. The city is known as the Paris of South America. It has everything you could want from a major metropolis but without the high costs of European cities. Living costs are low for those with foreign currency and you can live like a king for a fraction of the cost of doing so in the US or Europe (although in recent years prices are catching up).

In short, Argentina is a fantastic place to live and invest.

6. How Safe Is Argentina?

This is a question I often hear. It can be split into two parts - how safe are any investments and how safe is the country from a personal safety point of view.

Property Rights

People have often heard stories about South America and how corrupt it can be in places. Naturally, they wonder about the safety of any investment in Argentina. What if the seller didn't really own a property they may buy and the true owner wants it back? What if the government seizes property belonging to foreigners? And a dozen other questions like these.

Firstly, the Argentine constitution dating from 1853 guarantees equal property rights (in the widest sense) to both nationals and foreigners. Thus people are guaranteed the right to be able to own, trade, buy or sell companies, real estate, stock and other physical property in Argentina regardless of whether they are an Argentinean citizen or a foreign national. The treatment of property for both nationals and non-national alike is equal under the law. Therefore, once you have title to an Argentinean asset it is yours to do with as you please. Title is guaranteed and no-one can take it from you.

Secondly, the system of property title registration works well in Argentina because every real estate transaction must go through a *notario publico* (notary public) and a central registration office that documents every single buy and sell. The registration office is similar to the Land Registry in the UK. The notary will check the title of the person selling against the registry records to ensure the seller is indeed the lawful owner. Once a buyer becomes the new owner their details are recorded in the registry, guaranteeing their title.

Personal Safety

By and large Argentina is a very safe country. Although corruption can be commonplace this doesn't really impinge on personal safety matters.

Generally speaking, Buenos Aires is quite safe, as are all cities in Argentina. You need to be alert, but that's true in any large city in the world.

There are poorer neighborhoods in the outer suburbs, which can be a bit rough. Foreigners are advised to take caution if visiting these areas, especially after dark (not that there's usually any reason for them to go there). But put this in context, most cities have areas where it's best not to venture - London and New York being no exceptions.

As long as you use basic common sense, Argentina is very safe.

7. Information About Argentina

Visas

It is not necessary to have a visa for the purposes of buying real estate. All that is important is that you are in Argentina legally (unless of course you've given someone a Power of Attorney to buy on your behalf, in which case you don't need to be in the country at all!)

Nationals from the following countries do not need a tourist or business visa to enter Argentina:

All EU countries, Australia, Canada, Japan and the US, Andorra, Barbados, Bolivia, Brazil, Chile, Colombia, Costa Rica, Croatia, Dominican Republic, Ecuador, El Salvador, Guatemala, Haiti, Honduras, Israel, Liechtenstein, Malta, Mexico, Monaco, New Zealand, Nicaragua, Norway, Panama, Paraguay, Peru, San Marino, Singapore, Slovenia, South Africa, Switzerland, Turkey, Uruguay, Vatican City, Venezuela and Yugoslavia (Serbia and Montenegro).

Nationals from the above list can stay in Argentina for up to 90 days with a passport valid for at least 6 months and a return ticket. A dated entry stamp is made in the passport on arrival, and cancelled by a corresponding stamp on leaving. In practice, proof of having a return ticket is never required.

Nationals from Hong Kong (British Nationals Overseas), Jamaica and Malaysia can enter without a tourist visa for stays of up to 30 days.

Nationals from all other countries need to apply for a tourist visa from their nearest Argentinean embassy or consulate.

The Complete Guide To Real Estate Investment In Argentina

Extensions for a further 90 days are possible for most nationals; for details contact your Consulate (or Consular section at Embassy) once in Buenos Aires. A fee is payable for this.

An alternative and fun way to extend a visa is to jump on the ferry at Buenos Aires and cross the Rio Plata to Montevideo, the capital of Uruguay. On returning to Buenos Aires you will be given another 90 day stamp in your passport. I know several non-residents who live in Buenos Aires on a permanent basis who simply pop over to Montevideo every three months to renew their visa in this way.

There is a separate chapter about residency and citizenship later in the book.

Note that from early 2010 Argentina started charging an entry fee to US, Canadian and Australian citizens, which is payable on arrival. The fee is based on reciprocity, and these nationals are charged what their governments charge Argentinean nationals to enter their countries. As of early 2011 this was US citizens US$140, Canadians US$70, and Australians US$100.

Language

The official language in Argentina is Spanish, known as *Castellano* by the locals. It's slightly different from the Spanish spoken in most countries, in that it is heavily slang-riddled and still uses the *vos* form of address for "you" singular, not *tu*. (The vos form died out in Spain in the Seventeenth Century.)

7. Information About Argentina

Most people do not speak English well, if at all, although nearly everyone will know a few basic words. Many younger people now learn English at school. With a bit of effort you are likely to find someone that understands you almost everywhere in the country.

Time Zone

The time in Argentina is GMT -3 hours for the whole year. There is no daylight saving time and there is only one time zone across the whole country.

Argentina uses military time, which means the time is given in 24 hour format - e.g. 7pm is 19:00hs. Often you will see the designation hs after a time, which is short for *horas*, meaning hours.

Population And Geography

The population of Argentina is a little over 38 million, of which about one third lives in the capital, Buenos Aires, and about half live in the province of Buenos Aires.

The majority of the population is descended from early Spanish and Italian immigrants and are mainly Caucasian or Hispanic (in the European sense). Approximately 10% of the people are of indigenous Indian or *mestizo* (mixed race) descent.

Argentina covers 1,083,000 square miles, or 2,776,890 square kilometres, spanning a wide range of topographies. The country is divided into 23 provinces and one federal district - *Capital Federal*, the heart of Buenos Aires. The provinces are further subdivided into *departmentos* or *partidos*. Each province or department may

The Complete Guide To Real Estate Investment In Argentina

have its own local rules and taxes and some of these could apply to real estate purchases or rental income in their jurisdictions.

Country Dialling Code

Argentina's country code for international phone and fax calls is +54.

Currency and Banks

The official currency is the Argentinean peso ($), comprised of 100 *centavos* (cents). Before the economic crisis of 2002 the peso was pegged 1:1 with the dollar, but is now free to float on the world market. Since 2003 it remained pretty stable at just over 3:1 to the US dollar, with minor fluctuations but never more than a few cents. However in the last few years there's been a gradual downward drift and by early 2011 it stood at just over 4:1 (6.4:1 to the British pound (£)).

Occasionally prices are quoted in US dollars - this is usually only for certain imported goods and travel services, such as flights. The overwhelming majority of things are priced in pesos.

Most banks have ATMs (*Cajero Automatique*) which are linked to the Visa and Cirrus/Mastercard networks, so most foreign bank and credit cards can be used to withdraw local currency. Some ATMs also dispense dollars.

It is the law in Argentina that when using a credit card to purchase good or services ID must be presented. You will therefore need your passport when using one.

7. Information About Argentina

All banks will change foreign currency into pesos, however because of the bureaucratic way the system operates you will need to take your passport and stand in line for ages (see the banking chapter). You may also have to fill in a form. If you have US dollars a far easier way to change them is to make a purchase in one of the big supermarket chains, like *Carrefour* or *Disco*. You can pay in US dollars and receive your change in pesos. The exchange rate used is usually as good as that offered by the banks.

8. Real Estate In The Capital - An Overview

As previously explained, this book for the most part assumes that investors are going to be buying an apartment in central Buenos Aires, as this is what the overwhelming majority of foreigner buyers purchase.

The city of Buenos Aires is made up of two parts - the *Capital Federal* (CF) and *Gran Buenos Aires* (GBA). The CF is an autonomous region in the heart of the city. This was the original Buenos Aires city, which was federalized in the nineteenth century to differentiate it from the wider province of Buenos Aires in which it lay. The city limits included the former towns of Belgrano and Flores which are now districts in the city.

As the city grew over time it spread out far beyond the original city limits into Buenos Aires province. Metropolitan Buenos Aires today has 24 administrative divisions in the province, known as Gran (Greater) Buenos Aires. Although they form part of the modern city they are administered completely separately from the CF which is run by a different administration.

Note that sometimes the term GBA is used generically to refer to the whole city including the CF. In this book Buenos Aires is used to indicate the Capital Federal unless otherwise indicated.

Most of GBA consists of the poorer residential neighborhoods, and some can be quite rough. It also includes industrial areas. With the exception of the Northern Suburbs, GBA is not somewhere that buyers should really consider investment.

The Capital Federal, on the other hand, definitely is. It is certainly the nicer part of the city, with many parks and old

8. Real Estate In The Capital - An Overview

buildings. It is the cultural heart of the city. Although it only makes up about 6% of the whole of metropolitan Buenos Aires, the CF still covers an area of 77 square miles (200 sq km) and has a population of 2.8 million living in its 48 *barrios* (neighborhoods). The better off live in the CF and most people would live here if they could.

By and large the CF is arranged on a grid system, although some roads do bend a bit so it's not a true grid. Typically the blocks between the streets are more or less square-shaped, with each side being around a hundred metres in length, although some variation does occur. Each side of a block is usually made up of between two and six buildings (*edificios*).

Buildings are not numbered sequentially with reference to the street they are on, but sequentially relating to the block number on that street. For example, the first building of the twentieth block on Santa Fe will be numbered 2000. The next will be building 2002, its neighbor 2004, and so on. Odd and even numbers run down opposite sides of the street. The last building on block twenty may be 2010 - the next building won't be 2012 because it's on the next block - it will be number 2100.

Sometimes building numbers may be missing within the sequence, for example building 1520 may be next door to 1560. This is because originally there were other buildings here which took the missing numbers, but they have been knocked down at some point and the site redeveloped.

Block numbering starts from the same end for all streets running in the same direction - away from Av. Rivadavia (street

25

names change on crossing Av. Rivadavia) for what are roughly the north-south streets, and from the center (the river) for the east-west cross streets. Parallel streets carry the same block numbers, so for example turning off Santa Fe on the corner of block 15 will bring you to the corner of block 15 on Alvear, the next street. Block numbers run contiguously along cross streets. (Because it isn't quite a true grid system there are a few anomalies, but for the vast majority of time this is correct.) Once you have become familiar with the system it's quite easy to gauge where something is located based on its address.

The majority of block corners have street signs. As well as showing the name of the street, most will also tell you the range of building numbers that can be found on that block.

Most buildings are residential, although some office blocks do exist, most notably in the center (*centro*) - which isn't in the true center at all as the city is asymmetrical because of the Rio Plata.

Many buildings have stores (shops) or light commercial units (e.g. hairdressers) at street level, with residential units starting from the floor above, although this isn't always the case.

The number of stories an individual building has will vary, although for historical reasons eight floors (plus street level) is very common. Some will have many more than this.

Each unit within a building is owned by an individual owner. Collectively, the unit owners have the power to appoint a building manager to run the building on their behalf. He does so for an agreed monthly fee. This manager is known as the *administracion*,

8. Real Estate In The Capital - An Overview

or the administrator. The owners have the power to sack the administrator if they are unhappy with his performance.

The administrator takes responsibility for running the building. He will pay the bills for the running costs - elevators, electricity, cost of heating and hot water, and the caretaker's salary. He will also organize any necessary building repairs and instigate measures for preventative maintenance.

The running costs will be recouped (in practice this will be in advance) through the *expensas*, a monthly bill sent to each owner that details the expenditure. Obviously it depends on the actual building, but expensas are likely to be in the range of US$100 - US$200 per month and there is usually little variation between consecutive months. If a building has luxury facilities like a pool or a gym then the expensas will naturally be higher.

Each building will also have a *porteria*, which translates to concierge. As a bare minimum the porteria will act as a caretaker for the building. He will operate and maintain the plant, clean the communal areas and empty the garbage areas on each floor. Depending on the building and the terms of employment, the porteria may also act like a security guard or receptionist and may spend much time sitting at a desk in the building's lobby during stipulated hours, normally 8am to 8pm.

The porteria will live in the building. Usually the porteria's accommodation takes the form of a small apartment up on the roof next to the elevator heads, or at street level. The porteria is available during agreed hours, often on a 24 hour basis. At weekends a relief porteria may come in. Often, the porteria's wife will offer to do the residents' laundry at a reasonable rate to earn extra income.

Real estate is priced in Argentina by the square metre. A square metre is 10.8 square feet. Almost all property transactions are in cash - US dollars.

Since 2008 new regulations mean a permit is now required from AFIP (the Argentinean tax office) before a property can be legally put on the market for sale. The seller declares how much the sale price should be, and the permit allows the sale of that property within a given margin of the stated value. The new regulations require all sales to be reported to AFIP by the realtor and notary. If the reported sale price is outside of what AFIP consider an acceptable margin in relation to the permit price then the tax office may investigate the transaction. This is designed to stop under-reporting of the sale price and hence future asset tax payable, and reduces the scope for transactions to be done in "black" (i.e. not fully legally).

9. Buying a Home versus Buying For Investment

Before you start looking for property, it's absolutely crucial that you understand exactly why you want to buy a property in Argentina. The two main reasons people have are:

i). as an investment, and/or

ii). as a place to live yourself, either as a primary residence or a second home overseas

These two do not necessarily go hand in hand, although mistakenly people often think they do. In general the criteria for choosing a home and for choosing an investment property are different, although they can sometimes overlap. A mistake made by many investors is looking at real estate as if it were to become their personal residence. An investment usually should not be viewed as the investor's home.

When buying an apartment to rent out, particularly to tourists on short-term lets, the criteria for choosing the right apartment in the right location are very different to those you would probably have if you wanted to live in the property yourself.

The two main factors to consider are:

i). Location

Most short-term rental properties are located in the same areas as the four and five star hotels; principally Recoletta, Puerto Madero, Palermo and parts of Barrio Norte. These areas are effectively the heart of the city center (sometimes referred to as downtown). Most of the tourist attractions are located here. Whilst these areas are smart and safe, and undoubtedly nice areas to live in, they tend to be more expensive. Almost all properties in these areas are apartments, not houses.

On the other hand there are many other perfectly respectable neighborhoods in Buenos Aires which are perfectly nice to live in, especially if you have a family. Being a little further out from the main downtown area there is more choice of houses as well as apartments. Areas include Palermo Chico, Palermo Soho and Belgrano. These areas are significantly cheaper than central downtown so you'll get far more bang for your buck. However, these are not the best neighborhoods for short-term tourist rentals, although there can be a good demand for long-term rentals in these areas.

People often make the mistake of buying with their heart, not their head. They see an amazing building or apartment in a great area that they love, but that doesn't necessarily make a good investment. Buying a property because you have fallen in love with it, or because it has the attributes you like, without examining the underlying economics can potentially be a costly mistake. By the same token if you are looking to invest you should not necessarily pass on a property because it is in an ugly building or because the amenities you personally would like are lacking.

Another aspect of location is to consider the demographics of the people living in an area. Districts like Las Canitas are considered fashionable and trendy and attract a predominantly young crowd. Consequently, the kind of person most likely to be

9. Buying A Home versus Buying For Investment

interested in staying there is someone young and trendy, but often they can't afford a luxury apartment. Luxury apartments are therefore harder to rent out there.

Likewise, San Telmo is considered a quaint neighborhood, with its seen-better-days colonial architecture. It's mostly populated by students living in cheap apartments and people coming to learn tango. As such, it's unlikely to appeal to businessmen, so again luxury apartments will be harder to rent. However, property here is much cheaper and there is potentially a lot of scope for capital appreciation, particularly as the area is starting to be regenerated. There is potential here for buying and renting a cheap apartment, but this is a very different market to the luxury one.

Puerto Madero is an area which is always pushed hard by realtors. The old port area is being completely redeveloped, with scores of new apartment buildings going up, and many more planned. As it is new-build it's very expensive, and per square metre buyers can pay double what they do in parts of Recoleta, traditionally considered the most expensive district. The new concrete is rather soulless and the area currently has no character. Apart from the construction sites and the gleaming new apartment buildings, there's little else at present apart from a few hotels and restaurants. There are no shops and it's hard to find taxis. Despite the abundance of new-build property on sale, in short it probably isn't a good area to invest in currently, even if the prices weren't so sky-high. However, once all the construction projects are finished and the area reaches maturity (predicted for 2013) it may well have some serious real estate potential.

The Complete Guide To Real Estate Investment In Argentina

It's often said that the three most important things in real estate are (i) LOCATION (ii) LOCATION AND (ii) LOCATION. This is just as true in Buenos Aires and Argentina as it is in any other part of the world.

ii). Size

Most short-term rentals tend to be from seven days to two weeks. The people renting are probably doing so as an alternative to staying in a hotel - it's cheaper and they get a bigger space than a hotel room. For comparison, the average upscale hotel room is typically 25 - 30 square metres, so for the short time they are staying a 40 square metre plus studio or larger one or two bed apartment is fine, they probably won't want or need anything larger.

On the other hand, if you were to live in a 40 square metre apartment full time you would probably find it quite small, especially if you have a family. The size of the property is therefore crucial in relation to your purpose in buying it. As a rule of thumb if you personally are going to live in the apartment for three or more months a year then you should consider buying with your heart, not your head.

Some people buy as an investment with the idea of using the property themselves a few times a year for vacations. In this case they are not going to be spending the bulk of their time living there, so whilst in a sense it's a second home it is nevertheless important to consider size with respect to the majority period when it will be rented out. Nevertheless, people often think they need something larger so all the family can fit, but the real question is how often will

9. Buying A Home versus Buying For Investment

they actually bring all the family to stay in it? The answer is possibly never. If the answer is once or twice a year, consider what size of accommodation you normally stay in with all the family when you go on vacation - as often as not it will just be a hotel room or a small/medium-sized apartment. Why should your place in Buenos Aires be any different?

Many people in this situation make the mistake of buying something too big which doesn't maximize their rental potential. As property is priced per square metre obviously a bigger apartment will cost more. As a general rule, for the luxury rental market you shouldn't buy anything over 85 square metres, as you are unlikely to get a significant increase in the rent and indeed a really big apartment may prove much harder to rent.

So, to recap: the first question is for you to be absolutely clear in your own mind about whether you are buying real estate to live in personally or as an investment opportunity. Depending on which it is, factors such as size and location will be completely different and will need to be considered accordingly.

10. Buying as a Private Individual versus Buying As a Corporation

Almost certainly the answer to this question will be to buy as an individual, for the simple reason that when you come to sell the property there is no capital gains tax to pay (although if an individual buys and sells many times he may be deemed to be running a business and be taxed accordingly). Corporations, on the other hand, face a 35% capital gains charge.

However, there may be valid reasons related to your particular circumstances why it may be beneficial to buy a property through a corporation. Usually, this would be where future ownership will be complex and liable to alter. Shares in corporations can be sold or transferred, so whilst the legal ownership of the underlying real estate doesn't change (it is owned by the corporation), the ownership of the corporation itself can change through the redistribution of stock.

A typical use of this might be where a parent wants to pass future ownership of a property to a child, for example (but not on death - see below). Giving the property outright to the child at a later date may trigger a tax liability in the home country, but many countries allow gifts up to a certain value to be made annually without incurring a tax penalty. In the UK, for example, a person may give away as a gift up to £3,000 per annum tax free (provided they live for another seven years, else the gift will be counted for inheritance tax purposes).

By owning the property through a corporation it is possible to give away stock each year up to the permitted limit without

Buying As a Private Individual versus Buying As a Corporation

incurring a tax liability. Thus over time it may be feasible to pass complete ownership to ones children, tax free, via the transfer of stock. For this to be a considered option you need to check the specific tax rules applicable to your home country.

The other advantage to using a corporation are when two or more people want to own property jointly, perhaps business partners, and there is an intention to change the relative holdings over time. Again, the reasons for doing this must be overriding as it is perfectly possible to list more than one person on the title deed, and the ownership of the property doesn't have to be in equal shares.

As well as the capital gains tax issue, there are other downsides to using a corporation as the property ownership vehicle. As with corporations in all countries, it is necessarily to keep accurate books and records and to file annual returns. Whilst doing so is not particularly expensive in Argentina, nevertheless it does still cost something and there is also the time factor to consider. Depending on the complexity you will probably need to employ an accountant.

As already stated, the biggest issue about using a corporation is the 35% capital gains tax liability that will be incurred on sale of the property. (There isn't an actual capital gains tax, but the gain is treated as company income and corporate income tax is charged on it at 35%). However, this will only be an issue when you come to sell. If there are plans to hold onto the property indefinitely and it produces a good revenue stream then potential CGT issues may not be important. When it is finally time to sell (or for your executors

35

to sell), there may be things that can be done to mitigate the amount of tax paid, for example expenses that can be set against the increase in value. Also, it may be possible to offset the gain against any capital losses that have been made, and with clever use of double taxation treaties it may be possible to offset the gain against loses in your home country. This is something for tax experts to determine at the time of sale - tax laws change all the time in different countries and it is impossible to predict now what the possibilities for tax reduction will be.

If the property will be run as a business (e.g. a farm or vineyard) then there may be liability issues if the business should fail. Ownership through a company can mitigate the personal liability of the owner.

Corporations that can buy property can either be local Argentinean companies or foreign companies registered as such in the Public Register of Commerce. Both are briefly discussed below:

Local Argentinean Companies

Starting a corporation in Argentina is much like starting a corporation in most countries, only the process is a lot more bureaucratic. According to the legislation concerning company formation in Buenos Aires the following fifteen distinct steps are needed:

i). Getting the name verified by the Office of Corporations (*Inspección General de Justicia - IGJ*).

ii). *Certifying signatures of quota (stock) holders by a notary public*

Buying As a Private Individual versus Buying As a Corporation

iii). Obtaining a bank account in the name of the company to certify that 25% of the subscribed capital is paid-in.

iv). Publishing the new company's notice in the official paper (Boletín Oficial).

v). Payment of the incorporation fee

vi). Registration at the Registro Público de Comercio at the Inspection General de Justicia (IGJ).

vii). Purchase of special books.

viii). Submission of special books by a notary public for rubrication (i.e. to have the pages legally stamped in official red ink) by the IGJ.

ix). Obtaining a tax identification number (CUIT) from the National Tax Office (Administración Federal de Ingresos Públicos, AFIP).

x). Obtaining a social security number from AFIP.

xi). Registration of turnover tax at local level at the Dirección General de Rentas (DGR), in the City of Buenos Aires.

xii). Registration with the Unified System for Labor Registration (USLR).

xiii) Contraction of insurance for employees with a Risk Labor Company (Aseguradora de Riesgos del Trabajo - ART).

xiv). Registration with AFJPs (Aseguradoras de Fondos de Jubilaciones y Pensiones)

xv). Rubrication of wage books in the Ministerio de Trabajo (Ministry of Labor)

Some of these latter steps are unlikely to be relevant to a small corporation that just owns a property (e.g. if it doesn't employ staff), however the bureaucracy dictates that the relevant paperwork must still be filed. Company formation is not so much difficult as time consuming. It is estimated that on average it takes about a month to create a company, at a total cost of about US$600. If you are going to form a one I recommend that you hire a local lawyer (*abogado*) with experience in company formation to create it for you, as they will take care of all the details and ensure the correct procedures are followed.

Registered Foreign Companies

For a foreign company to buy property in Argentina it must be registered at the Public Register of Commerce (IGJ) as a foreign company.

There are two kinds of Incorporations of a Foreign Company:

i). A company which is going to set up a local company or buy an existing company and develop commercial activities through that local company.

Registration usually takes at least a month and the following documents have to be filed:

i). Certificate of Good Standing

ii). Articles of Incorporation/ Bylaws

iii). Certificate of Incorporation

iv). Annual report closing date

v). Current balance sheet

vi). Detailed shareholder information. The Shareholders of the foreign company must be individualized. If the Company has issued

Buying As a Private Individual versus Buying As a Corporation

bearer shares, the secretary or the President must issue certification that individualizes the shareholders. If the Company has issued nominative shares a notarized copy of the records of the company where the shareholders are registered must be supplied

vi). Evidence of the company's capacity to perform its activity in its country of origin, and proof that it does

vii). Legal statement from the company lawyer, indicating the corporate laws and regulations applicable to the foreign company (national and state), and that the company is able and has the capacity to perform its activity in its local country

viii). Minutes of the Board of Directors decision to incorporate the company in Argentina as a foreign company

ii). A company which desires to perform commercial activities directly in Argentina (e.g. as a branch)

Incorporation again takes about a month. The same documents as above have to be filed, along with details of the company's assets in both its country of origin and other countries.

The following rules apply to both types of company:

a). It is forbidden to incorporate companies which are not allowed to conduct business in their country of origin (i.e. offshore companies)

b). Foreign companies must really exist in their country of origin and not just have a seal of convenience.

The Complete Guide To Real Estate Investment In Argentina

c). The main purpose of the foreign company must not be to develop activities in Argentina

d). The company cannot be brand new. It must show assets, purposes, and other kinds of activity outside Argentina

e). The Company cannot be an investment fund

f). Registered companies must also be registered at the AFIP and have a valid tax number

The cost of registering a foreign company in Argentina is at least US$700. Again, if you are going to register a foreign company I recommend that you hire a local lawyer to do it on your behalf.

Unless you have very good reasons for doing otherwise, I strongly suggest that *you buy property as a private individual*. I cannot state this strongly enough.

The only downside (indeed it may even be an upside) in buying property as a private individual is that under Argentinean inheritance law, if you were to die the property would almost certainly pass to your next of kin - your spouse and children. You would not be able to cut your family out of your Argentinean property interests. Further details can be found in the *Death And Inheritance* chapter.

Note that property can be jointly owned by several people, and that their relative shareholdings do not have to be equal. This will be recorded on the property title.

11. Using a Property Investment Consultant versus Going It Alone

Should you use one of the growing band of property/investment consultants, or can you do everything you need to on your own to acquire your property? This is a good question, and the answer is: it all depends.

There are many firms in Buenos Aires that profess to offer real estate consultancy services. Some are little more than out-and-out cowboys, who will take your money - often an exorbitant fee - and do little more than point you in the direction of their pet realtor, who is possibly corrupt and certainly won't have your interests at heart.

Other consultancy firms are more genuine and will provide a lot more help in sourcing a property and helping you negotiate the price. Beware though that they may well have a hidden agenda - they may point you to a realtor that gives them a backhander, and if they charge a percentage fee they have a vested interest in seeing that you don't get the best deal (despite claiming otherwise) as it makes their fee bigger.

Most consultants I've come across have some sort of scam going on somewhere so they (or their business associates) can cream off more from you along the line. They may not tell outright lies, but often they may not tell you all the facts you need to know to make a rational investment decision. I've come across several people who have used consultancy firms who were not told about the annual property tax they would have to pay later, or who were recommended to a dodgy lawyer who charged phantom property taxes which were not applicable on a first purchase. Claims about potential rental income are often exaggerated as are claims about typical occupancy rates.

Consultants may be part of realtor and/or rental agency companies, and although they may claim to offer independent advice they may try to suck you into using their company's services, which may not be in your best interests. In short, there's a potential army of people waiting to take advantage of you if you let them.

Before using any consultant, it is crucial to ascertain that they can speak English to a reasonably high standard (unless you are fluent in Spanish), as this is essential to make sure your requirements are clear and to avoid misunderstandings. Depending on the linguistic ability of the consultant's contacts, he may have to act as an interpreter between you and other parties.

A good consultant will be independent, or if he works for an employer (e.g. a realtor) will be honest and upfront about this. A good consultant should help you at every step of the way, including helping you identify your exact requirements, helping you identify potential properties in the areas you are interested in, giving impartial advice about valuation and rental potential and helping negotiate the purchase price. The good consultant will also have an excellent network of contacts that they have built up over time, including reputable realtors and ethical *escribanos* (property lawyers). They should be able to recommend to you a choice from which you can select the ones you feel most comfortable with, without undue pressure.

Using a Property Investment Consultant versus Going It Alone

The consultancy process doesn't have to end when the property is purchased. You may need advice on such things as refurbishment, suitable furnishings and fittings for renting the place out, helping in choosing a rental agency, changing services into your name, and any one of a number of post-purchase issues. A good consultant should also be able to help you with all these things in the same professional manner. Here again, there is scope to be ripped off if the consultant recommends tradesmen he is in with who will overcharge foreigners, who are less likely to be aware of the going rates for work and materials.

Despite the many consultancy cowboys, there are a few good consultancy firms out there, but they are not cheap. Typically you can expect to pay upwards of US$4,000 for help with sourcing and buying a property. Usually, the fee is payable upfront and valid for help and advice over a twelve month period. Sometimes, a percentage is charged.

Some firms, particularly those targeted at North Americans, offer a complete service where the investor signs a Power of Attorney and the agency will source, negotiate and buy a suitable investment property, without the investor ever needing to set foot in Argentina. They will then rent out and manage the property on the investor's behalf. Personally, I would never dream of buying a property I had never seen, but I have met people who have done it, and surprisingly it has usually turned out ok. If you are going to use a service like this (and I don't recommend that you do), then take very great care to research the agency extremely thoroughly as you are giving them authority to buy a property on your behalf. You don't want to be sold a duff place that no-one else will touch. Always, always insist on seeing references from existing clients and try to speak to as many as you can.

For the post-purchase side, the best consultancy firms charge upwards of US$4,000 for full project management for property refurbishment. Post-purchase consultancy is usually also available on a per-time basis, but the rates vary widely. I've seen some quoted rates as high as US$350 per hour.

So, back to the original question of do you need a consultant? It depends on a number of factors, including how comfortable you are with the language, how much you want to do yourself and how much you want others to do for you.

It is perfectly possible to do everything yourself without using a consultant. First you need to find a reliable realtor that speaks good English (if your Spanish is non-existent or poor). See the later chapter on realtors for further details. The realtor will help you find the property you want (although watch out for the usual scams). Once you've found a property and negotiated a price you will need to choose and appoint an escribano to handle the legal side. Here again the realtor may be able to help you. It isn't difficult, but the key is making sure the people you select to work with are honest and reliable.

On the other hand, you may feel more comfortable letting someone else do most or all of the work for you. This could include viewing suitable properties on your behalf and making an offer, or merely helping you select suitable properties that you can view

Using a Property Investment Consultant versus Going It Alone

yourself, and giving advice on how much to offer. A good consultant could save you more than the cost of their fees.

If you decide you do need to use a consultant, then how much or how little that consultant does for you should be entirely your decision. You should only do what you feel comfortable doing, and let a professional do the rest. When appointing a consultant it's important to bear in mind the earlier points about people all too keen to part you from your money, and to perform due investigation on the company. Check all references and ask around. It's your money you will be paying so you owe it to yourself.

The supplementary appendix to this book contains details of real estate investment consultants that are known to be reliable and honest, along with a guide to their current fee rates.

12. The Return on Investment (ROI)

If you are looking to purchase real estate for investment purposes, you need to take into account the potential Return on Investment (ROI).

The return on investment is the rate of return of money on your investment. It is the ratio of money gained (or lost) on an investment in relation to the amount of money invested, and is normally expressed as a percentage.

To illustrate with a simple example, if an investment costs $100,000, and annually gives a income of $5,000, then the ROI is $5,000 divided by $100,000 which gives an ROI (or yield) of 5%.

ROI can also be referred to as rate of profit, yield, or just plain simple return.

For our purposes, ROIs will be used to compare the rate of return on different investments. All things being equal, an investment that gives an ROI of 10% is a better investment (better utilisation of your capital) than one which has an ROI of say 9%.

ROI, from a strictly mathematical point of view, can be very complex, involving many complicated equations used to work out annualized returns where income streams occur monthly or sporadically, or that take into account the time value of money and how it will be worth less in future. These topics are beyond the scope of this book and are not necessary for our purposes. All we need is a simple percentage figure for comparison as in the example above.

To work out the ROI for a property you are interested in you must first work out the total cost if you were to buy it. This isn't just

12. The Return On Investment (ROI)

the purchase price the vendor is paid, you must also add all the other costs associated with the purchase. These include consultancy fees (if applicable), realtor and escribano fees, and property taxes (if applicable). Typically these will add at least six plus percent (quite likely more) over and above the actual selling price.

If your property will need refurbishment you should include as accurately as possible the predicted costs related to the refurbishment, including (if necessary) project management fees, costs of materials and labor etc.

The sum of the above costs is your total cost figure for acquiring your investment and getting it into a position where you can start generating a revenue stream. To calculate the ROI you need to know what annual revenue your property will generate after all costs have been deducted.

You start with a base cost - your predicted annual rent. Your consultant or realtor should be able to give you a guide - if not go and talk to some rental agencies. If you are serious about buying property you will already have gotten a good feel about market rates by this time.

Treat the figures you are given with caution, sometimes agents talk up market rates to try and get your business. By giving a higher figure compared to what another agent tells you they think they can get for your property, an agent will hope that you will naturally choose them as they will get you more. The same thing tends to happen in property markets all over the world. In Buenos Aires it generally isn't too bad, but it's something you need to be aware of.

A bigger problem than inflating the likely rent is downplaying the unoccupancy period. The unoccupancy period is the time when you have no tenants - i.e. between rentals. It's common to be quoted occupancy rates of 90% or more by people keen to sell you a property or engage your business. The reality is that depending on the property the occupancy is very likely to be less than this.

It's impossible to accurately predict occupancy periods. They tend to be based on the property itself and how it is marketed in comparison to other properties. A lot depends on the agent. The demand may also vary a little on a seasonal basis. (Occupancy periods are covered in more detail in the *Choosing a Rental Agent* chapter.) As a rule of thumb, I tend to use an occupancy rate of 70% for short-term rentals, or assume a vacancy period of one to three months between long-term lets, when doing my calculations. It may not be totally accurate, but it's generally a good yardstick.

To get the gross annual income figure, first calculate the rent on an annual basis (e.g. if you have been given a monthly rental figure, multiply it by twelve). Then multiply it by your predicted occupancy percentage to give the likely gross rental income.

You now need to work out the net income figure - this is the gross rental income minus all expenses incurred in the day to day running of the property. These include agency fees, building fees (expensas), insurances and costs of repairs etc. What you are left with is your gross profit.

The gross profit divided by your total cost for acquiring the property gives you the predicted ROI for that property. This can be used as a basis for comparing different properties.

12. The Return On Investment (ROI)

If you intend to take out a loan or mortgage in your home country to fund your property purchase in Argentina, then you should include notional interest payments in the costs you deduct from the gross rental income. If you are left with a negative figure then you will make a loss on this investment, and your ROI will be negative. In this case I would recommend staying well clear and not buying (although some people may still be attracted by the capital appreciation potential).

If you are borrowing some of the purchase funds an alternative way of looking at the return takes into account that you will have in reality invested less capital. For example, on a US$100,000 property a US$5,000 income gives a yield of 5%, but if you've only put down US$20,000 and borrowed the other 80% then the costs of borrowing reduce this income to (say) US$2,000. This changes the calculation to give a 10% ROI on your original US$20,000 investment. This in-depth analysis starts to get complicated and is mentioned for reasons of completeness, but can be ignored for comparison purposes.

For your own purposes, you may wish to deduct tax payable on your rental earnings to produce an ROI after tax. However, for comparison purposes again this tax can be considered a constant and can be ignored.

An ROI calculation will inevitably make many assumptions. It is therefore a good idea to build a spreadsheet model where you can try changing those assumptions to see what affect each has on the predicted ROI.

The Complete Guide To Real Estate Investment In Argentina

It would be useful to show here a complete ROI calculation for a sample property. However, as many of the costs and expenses haven't been explained yet the sample calculation is given later in the book where it will make more sense. At this stage it is just important to know that you need to take ROI into consideration before buying a place, and what it is.

ROI is important, but it isn't the only factor to consider when deciding whether to purchase a property. It is merely a useful guide. A property with an ROI of 7% that you really like might be just as good an investment as a property that doesn't feel as good but has an ROI of say 8%. After all, predicting rents and occupancy isn't an exact science and the predicted ROI is just that, a prediction. (Of course if you already own the property and have been renting it out then you can work out an accurate ROI for the past period, but that's a different matter.) Don't use ROI in isolation in deciding whether to buy, consider other factors as well.

Finally, you should consider the potential for the utilisation of your capital on another asset class. If you can get a rate of return of say 9% by buying a property in Argentina, but can buy another kind of investment elsewhere with an ROI of say 15%, then you should consider if that would not perhaps be a better home for your money. (Of course this may be complicated by capital appreciation issues.)

13. Choosing Areas of Buenos Aires To Invest In

The south of the Capital Federal is less wealthy and developed than the north (Recoleta, Barrio Norte, Palermo, Belgrano, etc). Puerto Madero (the docklands) is an exception and is now one of the most expensive areas of the city.

This division has historical reasons. In the 19th century the south was the best part of the city, but was struck by a yellow fever epidemic in the 1850's so everybody who could afford it moved north away from the water and the port where the epidemic began. The north has ever since remained the wealthy part and this divide continues up to the present day.

Santa Fe Avenue is one of the main dividing lines - to the south of Santa Fe will be cheaper, to the north and east more expensive. Of course, as elsewhere, the greatest capital appreciation is often going to be found in the up-and-coming districts.

It's not just the district that determines whether a property will be a good investment. Factors such as being on a side street, the floor level and how far the property is from the main avenues like Santa Fe, Alvear, Callao, etc. and from the *subte* (metro/subway/underground) system all come into play.

Many investors buy for short-term rentals (serviced apartments). If this is the case it doesn't make sense to pay top dollar per square metre for an apartment in the best part of Recoleta when you can pay half of that a few blocks away. The average tourist that books an apartment won't know a difference of five or six blocks.

The Complete Guide To Real Estate Investment In Argentina

Properties in the north of the city start at around US$1,400 per square metre, whilst in areas such as San Telmo in the south they start at around US$950 (US$1,300 for new constructions).

Barrio Norte is an area that often comes up, but it doesn't actually exist on any maps. It is not technically a district but is the informal name given to the part of Buenos Aires centring around Santa Fe avenue, including parts of Retiro, Recoleta, Balvanera, and Palermo.

The main districts out of the Capital Federal's 48 barrios that will be of interest to the real estate investor are discussed below. Note that the prices given are typical as of early 2011 and may well have increased, perhaps significantly.

Recoleta

Recoleta is considered to be the most exclusive neighborhood in Buenos Aires; equivalent to Mayfair in London or New York's Upper East Side. It is an historic area much frequented by tourists and the city's residents for its cafés, galleries and the famous Recoleta cemetery where Eva Perón is buried.

Recoleta is an affluent residential district and is one of the most expensive places to live in Buenos Aires, both in terms of real estate and the cost of living. It is known as the Paris of the Americas. Many French-style palaces and villas have been built here and its verdant squares are known for their cafés and bars.

13. Choosing Areas of Buenos Aires To Invest In

Recoleta hosts one of the best (and expensive) hotels in Latin America, the five-star Hotel Alvear, along with a number of other upscale 4/5 star hotels. Close by are mansions built by the most important families of Buenos Aires, many now used as embassies. The area bustles with nightlife and the pedestrian passage RM Ortíz is renown for its restaurants.

Recoleta houses the upscale Buenos Aires Design mall, containing many shops that highlight the latest designs in homeware and interior design, drawing in affluent shoppers. Nearby are the National Library, the National Museum of Fine Arts and the University of Buenos Aires Law Faculty.

Recoleta undoubtedly contains some of the city's most sought-after real estate. Prices in this neighborhood start at US$1,800 per square metre and go up to US$3,500 or more. It is a particularly good area for short-term rentals.

Palermo

Palermo is located in the northeast of the city, bordering Belgrano to the north and and Recoleta to the south. With an area of 17.4 km² it is the largest neighborhood in Buenos Aires. Palermo contains the Botanical Gardens, the city airport (Aeroparque Jorge Newbery), several sport clubs, the Jardín Japonés (Japanese Garden) and the Galileo Planetarium as well as several other parks and open spaces.

The Complete Guide To Real Estate Investment In Argentina

Although it appears as one big swath on the map, Palermo can be subdivided into a number of contrasting and individual parts, each of which can be considered as de facto neighborhoods in their own right. These divisions are used on real estate descriptions and are identified below.

Alto Palermo (Villa Freud)

Alto Palermo is downtown Palermo, the main shopping area and transport hub around Av. Santa Fe. At its core is the Alto Palermo Shopping Center, a large shopping mall. Villa Freud, based around Plaza Güemes, is a residential area known for its high concentration of psychoanalysts and psychiatrists, hence its name.

Palermo Viejo

Palermo Viejo (Palermo old town) is the oldest part. Bounded by Av. Santa Fe, Av. Coronel Díaz, Av. Córdoba and Carranza street, the neighborhood is centered on Plaza Palermo Viejo and reflects an older Spanish style of architecture, mixed with modern elements. Such well-known figures as Jorge Luis Borges and Che Guevara once lived here. It was historically a residential area, popular with communities from Poland, Armenia, Ukraine and Lebanon and old Spanish and Italian families, whose traditions are reflected in local restaurants, churches, schools and cultural centers.

13. Choosing Areas of Buenos Aires To Invest In

Palermo Soho

Palermo Soho is a small area of Palermo Viejo around Plaza Serrano (officially Plazoleta Cortázar), and it is a newly-fashionable area for fashion, design, restaurants, bars and street culture. The atmosphere in many cafés and restaurants strives to be alternative, which makes this area of the city especially popular with young, upper-middle class Argentines as well as foreign tourists. The traditional low houses have been adapted into boutiques and bars, creating a bohemian feel. The square often hosts a crafts fair.

Palermo Hollywood

A newer area, Palermo Hollywood has become the media district of Buenos Aires. It is centered on the streets of Honduras and Fitzroy across the rail tracks from Palermo Viejo and, like nearby Palermo Soho, is a popular night-time destination for its bars and clubs.

Palermo Chico and Barrio Parque

Across Figueroa Alcorta Avenue, between San Martín de Tours and Tagle streets, Palermo Chico (small or exclusive) is the most upmarket part of Palermo. The Buenos Aires Museum of Decorative Arts is located in Palermo Chico in a dazzling old palatial home. Neighbouring Barrio Parque is strictly a residential area, laid out in winding streets. Many of the wealthy and famous own homes here. Once a quarter full of splendid mansions set in broad private parks, many luxury condominiums have now been built.

The Complete Guide To Real Estate Investment In Argentina

Las Cañitas

Las Cañitas was historically a slum area but is now an upmarket area of restaurants and bars next to the Campo Argentino de Polo in the extreme north of Palermo.

Real estate prices in Palermo are typically in the US$1,500 - US$2,400 per square metre range. The area is popular with tourists so is suitable for both long and short-term rentals.

Puerto Madero

Puerto Madero is the old port area. It is being completely redeveloped, with scores of new apartment buildings being constructed and many more planned. The new concrete is rather soulless and the area currently has little character. Apart from the construction sites and the gleaming new apartment buildings there's little else apart from a few hotels and restaurants. Despite the abundance of new-build property on sale, it probably isn't a good area to invest in currently, even if the prices weren't so high. However, once all the construction projects are finished and the area reaches maturity (predicted for 2013) it may well have some serious potential.

Puerto Madero is an area which is always pushed hard by realtors. Typically prices go from US$2,500 - US$3,300 per square metre. It is appropriate for both long and short-term rentals.

13. Choosing Areas of Buenos Aires To Invest In

Belgrano

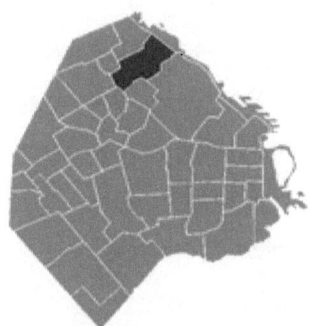

Belgrano is a leafy barrio to the north of Palermo. It is an upper-middle class neighborhood that can be roughly divided into Belgrano R, Belgrano C, central Belgrano, and Lower Belgrano. The heart of the Belgrano pulses with life on its main thoroughfare, Avenida Cabildo, which runs northwest to southeast and is followed by subte line D.

Belgrano C is home to Buenos Aires' small Chinatown and is crowded with restaurants and specialty grocery stores. Belgrano R is chiefly residential and low-density in nature, characterized by calm streets lined with large, mature shade trees. Most buildings are detached single-family homes and many some have sizable gardens with swimming pools. This section is favored by wealthy Argentineans and expatriate businessmen. Belgrano contains several lush parks that are particularly vibrant at weekends.

Real estate prices are typically US$1,500 - US$2,300. The area does not receive many tourists so it is more appropriate for long-term rentals.

The Complete Guide To Real Estate Investment In Argentina

Retiro

Retiro is in the north east, adjacent to Recoleta and north of Puerto Madero. It includes parts of the Santa Fe shopping district, San Martín square and the Retiro transportation hub with its train, subte, and main bus stations, always teeming with commuters during weekdays.

Retiro is a popular residential area for expatriate executives and tourists, and is therefore suitable for both long and short-term rentals. Prices are typically US$1,600 - US$2,700 per square metre.

San Telmo

San Telmo is one of the oldest neighborhoods of Buenos Aires and also one of the best preserved areas with a number of colonial houses and streets still paved with the original cobblestones.

San Telmo is the birthplace of tango and is now an artist's quarter with a bohemian feel. Before the yellow fewer epidemic it was once the most fashionable part of town; afterwards it became predominantly home to poor immigrants in cramped, divided quarters. Many of these crumbling old houses still exist. Attempts are being made to rejuvenate the area and it is considered up and coming.

13. Choosing Areas of Buenos Aires To Invest In

The main square, Plaza Dorrego, houses a semi-permanent antique fair (Feria de Antiguedades). The area's many other attractions include old churches, museums and antique shops, along with many restaurants and bars.

The area is popular with tourists and has a reputation for cheap accommodation, but is considered slightly dangerous at night. It is suitable for both long and short-term rentals. Prices are typically US950 - US$1,500 per square metre (up to US$1,600 for new construction).

Microcentro

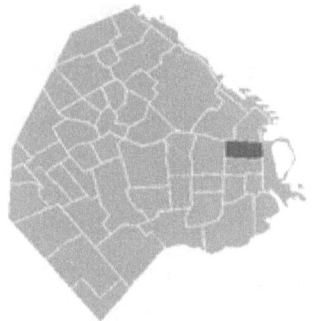

The microcentro lies within the barrios of San Nicolás and Montserrat, to the west of Puerto Madero. The city's major public buildings are found here, centered around Plaza de Mayo. Pedestrianized Av Florida is one of the capital's most fashionable shopping streets, filled to capacity during the day with bustling crowds of shoppers, tourists and businessmen. When people say downtown it's often the microcentro that they are referring to.

The area is ideal for both long and short-term rentals. Prices are typically US$1,600 - US$2,600 per square metre.

The Complete Guide To Real Estate Investment In Argentina

La Boca

La Boca is Buenos Aires' most colorful neighborhood.

It has a strong European flavor following the Italian immigrants who first settled here in less than ideal conditions. Today the barrio is partly an artist's quarter but is still mainly working class.

La Boca is a popular destination for tourists visiting Argentina, with its brightly-colored houses in the main street, the Caminito. Other attractions include the La Ribera theatre, many tango clubs and Italian taverns, as well as La Bombonera, home of The Boca Juniors, one of South America's top football clubs. La Boca can be rough in places and visitors are advised to take care if they stray from the riverside walk or the tourist section of Caminito.

Although parts of La Boca are visited by large numbers of tourists, it's not an area they stay in. Currently it is only really suitable for low-end, low-yield long-term rents, although it has been identified as a potential up and coming area and there may be excellent future capital gain opportunities for those brave enough to take the risk, although this is by no means guaranteed. Property prices are typically US$650 plus per square metre.

13. Choosing Areas of Buenos Aires To Invest In

The map below shows the main avenues and streets of the Capital Federal (image courtesy of Wikipedia).

The Complete Guide To Real Estate Investment In Argentina

Below is a map of Buenos Aires' subte system (image courtesy of Robert Schwandl, urbanrail.net).

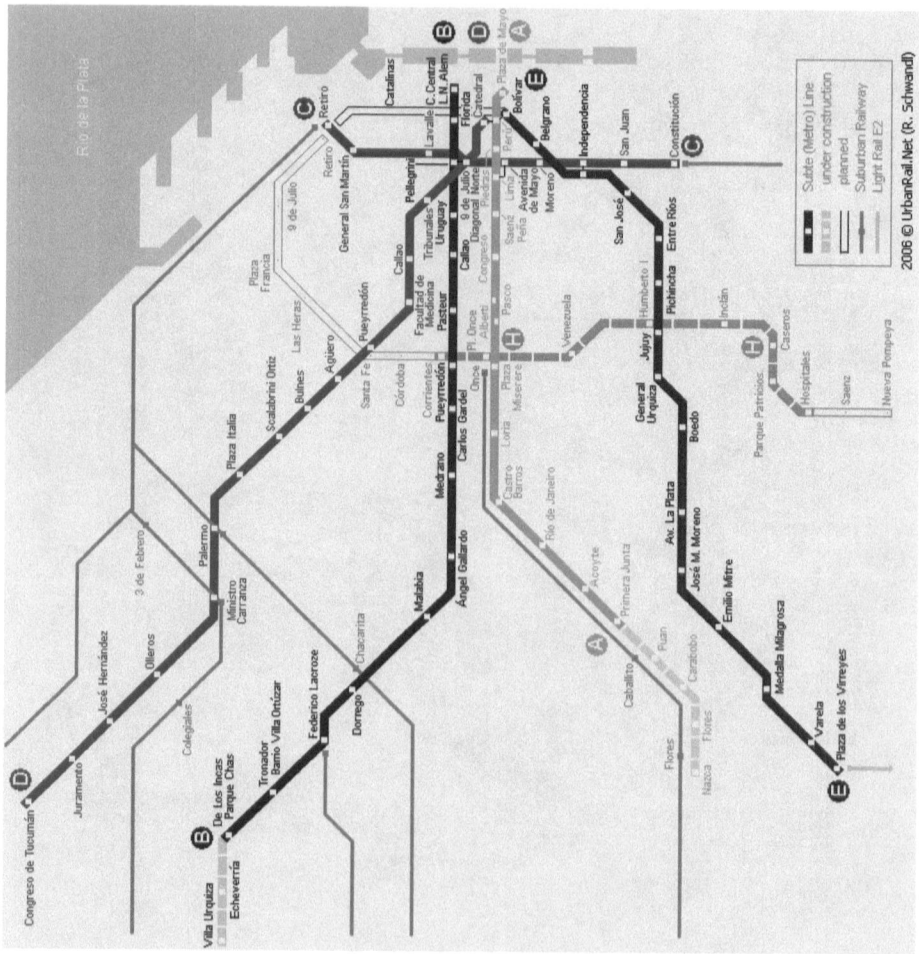

You can cross-reference both maps with the barrio outline drawings shown earlier.

14. Finding Suitable Property For Sale

There are two main ways of finding suitable property for sale in Buenos Aires. i) Newspapers, and ii) Realtors. The merits of each are explained below.

i). Newspapers:

The two main daily newspapers published in Buenos Aires are La Nacion and Clarin. Both have classified advertising sections containing properties for sale which are a good source of property listings, and both have websites which allow properties for sale to be searched online. Permitted search parameters include property type, number of rooms, district and price range.

Clarin's web site is located at http://www.inmuebles.clarin.com
La Nacion's is at http://clasificados.lanacion.com.ar

There is also the English language newspaper The Buenos Aires Herald, whose website is at http://www.buenosairesherald.com, although there is usually a lot less property advertised on this site, as published for the English-speaking community its circulation is much smaller.

Although not a newspaper, www.argenprop.com is another useful site containing property listings from various sources.

As well as the current adverts, the sites can return recent adverts such as those placed in the last week or month. Some adverts carry photos of the apartments and perhaps a floor plan,

The Complete Guide To Real Estate Investment In Argentina

but many don't. As well as private sellers, some realtors also advertise what's on their books on these pages.

At first many adverts may appear confusing, or look as if they are written in some kind of scientific notation. A typical advert may look something unintelligible like this:

Recoleta*: 3amb. cfte super lum lav bño y coc compl. Plac ptio 70m^2 impec bcón Beruti 1777 Dep 75 15°*

Once you understand how to read them these adverts will make perfect sense. They are written in Spanish (as they are written by locals for locals), so the key is to understand what the Spanish words mean. This isn't difficult, but it is made more complicated because often abbreviations are used.

The table below explains the main terms and their abbreviations that you are likely to encounter.

14. Finding Suitable Property For Sale

Term	Abbr	Explanation
aire acondicionado	ac	Air Conditioning
alquilado		Rented - the property has a tenant
ambientes	amb	The number of rooms in an apartment - note this isn't the same as the number of bedrooms, living rooms and dining rooms count as well. Hence a 3 amb apartment may consist of 2 bedrooms and a living area. 1 amb means a studio apartment
amplio/a	ampl	Wide
años	añ	Years - how many years old the apartment is - e.g. 50 añ
antiguo	antig	Old - The apartment is in an old building
bajas expensas	b/exp	Low monthly expenses (condo fee)
balcón	bcón	The apartment has a balcony
baño y cocina completos	bño y coc compl	Complete bathroom and kitchen i.e. all facilities present - bathroom has bath as well as shower, and kitchen has space and plumbing for all the usual white goods
calefaccion	calef	Heating
casa		The property is a house
cochera	coch	Includes parking space
comedor diario	c/drio	A room for daily dining - i.e. a dining room
contrafrente	cfte	At the back of the building (often quieter)
cubierto	cub	Covered area - i.e. inside

65

The Complete Guide To Real Estate Investment In Argentina

dep de servicio	servicio	The apartment has quarters for a maid
departamento	dep or dept	An apartment (in a block)
dormintorio	dor	Bedroom
edificio	ed	An apartment block or building
escritorio	esc	The apartment has an office or study
esquina	esq	Corner - often used in directions to show the nearest cross street to a block
excelente vista	exl vta	The apartment has a good view
frente	fte	At the front of the building
hermoso/a	herm	Beautiful
impeccable	impec	Impeccable or immaculate condition
jardin	jard	Garden
lateral	lat	On the side of the building
lavadero	lav	Laundry
living-comedor	lc	A combined living/dining area
luminoso	lum	The apartment gets a lot of light
metros cuadrados	mc	Square metres
mucama	muc	The building provides a maid service
parilla	par	The apartment has a built-in BBQ
patio	ptio	Patio or terrace
piscina	pisc	The building has a swimming pool
piso	p, ps	Floor within a building, e.g. 8th floor. Note that the numbering system is the same as that used by the British, not Americans (see below)

14. Finding Suitable Property For Sale

placard	plac	Wardrobe or closet (usually built in)
semipiso	semip	Half-floor or half-landing
todo nuevo	t/nvo	Brand new - can mean either the building or that the apartment has been completely refurbished
toilette	toil	Toilet, or washroom
ubicacion	ubic	The apartment is in an excellent location
ver	v	Looking over, or overlooking

So to get back to the example above, our advert reads:

Apartment in Recoleta, 3 rooms, at the back of the building, very light, laundry, complete kitchen and bathroom, built-in wardrobe, patio, 70 square metres in size, immaculate condition, balcony.

Beruti is the name of the street the apartment block is on, and it's at number 1777. Inside the block, the apartment is number 75, and is on the 15th floor. The street name is always given before the number - e.g. Beruti 1777.

The ground floor (i.e. street level) inside a building is known as the *Planta Baja*, often shown as PB, especially on elevator buttons. The first floor is the floor above the PB. This is the same numbering system that the British use, but is different from that used in North America where the street-level floor is known as the first floor or floor 1.

In Latin America, the degree sign 'º' is usually used to mean floor number. Thus 8º means the 8th floor. Although technically it's not needed the floor number is usually included as part of an address.

Adverts usually give the address of the apartment and a contact telephone number. You need to call the owner to make an appointment to view the property, which could be difficult if you don't speak much Spanish. It's very unlikely the person on the other end of the phone will speak any English. Speaking on the phone in a foreign language is much harder than face to face conversation. If you can, try to get someone who speaks Spanish to make the call on your behalf, otherwise you may have problems.

Argentineans tend to be quite security-conscious and it is possible that the owner will want a number to call you back on (preferably a landline, not a cell phone) to make the appointment. They may also want to meet you outside the property initially.

Many new-build constructions will employ security guards (who double as salesmen), and in these cases you will be able to visit apartments in the building without making an explicit appointment; the guard will show you round. This is usually indicated on the advert, or you will be told this when you phone.

In Buenos Aires many sellers will have an open day. Traditionally, open days are held on Saturday afternoons, but not always. The dates and times of any open day will be on the advert - e.g. something like Sab 09 15-17, which in this case means Saturday (*Sabado*) the 9th between 15:00 and 17:00 hours. An open day is when the property owner guarantees to be there to show people around, and interested parties can just turn up between the specified hours to view the property without making a

14. Finding Suitable Property For Sale

specific appointment. It is very common for potential buyers to view half a dozen or more properties on a hectic Saturday afternoon schedule.

Classified advertisers have the option of renewing their adverts until their property is sold, and knowing how long a property has been on the market can be useful. This can be determined by tweaking the date to search adverts from, and seeing if the property you are interested in still comes back in the search results. It's true that a property that has been on the market for a long time may be overpriced or have something fundamentally wrong with it (although not necessarily), but on the other hand the owner may be desperate to sell and could be amenable to a considerably lower offer.

ii). Realtors:

The role of a realtor is to help you find suitable property that matches your requirements, take you on viewings of that property, and to oversee the negotiation and purchase process. In this sense the role of the realtor is pretty much as it is in most places in the world. However, in Buenos Aires there are a few differences.

Firstly, both the buyer and seller pay realtor fees. Yes, the buyer as well. Fees are usually only paid on the contract signing (see later chapter), so if the realtor doesn't find you a property you won't pay anything. The standard fee for residential property is usually 3% (plus VAT) for both the buyer and seller, except in the suburbs of Buenos Aires where it's usually 2% for the seller and 4% for the buyer. With some realtors the fees can be higher. For

The Complete Guide To Real Estate Investment In Argentina

commercial property (except farms and vineyards, which are usually 3%) the buyer normally pays 4 or 5%. The fee is strictly non-negotiable, realtors would rather lose business than lose commission.

In Buenos Aires the buyer's commission is usually split 50/50 between the realtors, whilst in the rest of the country the buyer's realtor usually keeps it all.

Secondly, unlike European and North American realtors, realtors in Buenos Aires don't just show you what's on their books. They actually work for you - that's why the buyer pays a commission.

Buenos Aires realtors have properties on their books that they are trying to sell. Ideally they would like you to buy something on their books, that way they get both the seller's and buyer's commission. But the difference is if they don't have anything suitable on their books, or nothing that interests you, they will hunt for property that matches your requirements. They will contact other agents to see if they have suitable property, and if they have, they will set up appointments for you to view it. The realtor is actively working for you.

This is why it's vital to find a good realtor, and why unlike in other countries you only get involved directly with one realtor, not everyone in town.

For some reason realtors tend not to trust one another, and are guarded with their listings with respect to viewings. Often you will have the situation that when viewing the property not only will you

14. Finding Suitable Property For Sale

be there with your realtor, but the seller's realtor (and possibly the seller) will be present as well.

Realtors want to help you find the property you want so they can earn their commission. They don't care where these properties come from, so if you see a property for sale that you like the look of, take the realtor's details from the sale board and pass them on to your realtor. They will be more than happy to set up a viewing for you.

Likewise, if you like the sound of an advert in one of the newspapers, your realtor will be pleased to arrange a viewing.

Whilst it's not absolutely essential to use a realtor, without doubt they make finding a property much easier. Also many properties are only sold via a realtor, so by using one you are exposing yourself to the full range of what's on the market.

Personally, I consider the use of a realtor to be indispensable.

www.mapa.buenosaires.gov.ar

www.mapa.buenosaires.gov.ar provides a useful interactive map of the city. Enter a cross street and the map will zoom to that location and show the building outlines. Select the relevant tabs and click on the outline plan to bring up a photo of that building, along with useful information such as the barrio, nearest school and public transport links etc. It's also possible to overlay the map with aerial photos taken in 1940, 1965, 1978 and 2004. This is a useful tool to investigate the location of potential properties.

15. Choosing A Realtor *(inmobiliaria)*

In Spanish, realtors are known as *inmobiliaria*. Buenos Aires has hundreds of inmobiliaria and you will find one every few blocks. Some specialize in just sales and others in both sales and rentals. Most are not very good.

In theory every agency needs at least one licensed realtor, who will have completed a three-year university course to get their license. In most of Argentina this is well enforced, but not in downtown Buenos Aires where the realtor industry appears to be largely unregulated - it seems anyone can set themselves up as a realtor without any formal training or experience. Many realtors also employ staff that have no training or experience. These are not the people you want to be doing business with.

As the realtor will be working for you, it is critical that you select one that you can trust and that is honest and reliable. Language will probably be the biggest issue; very few realtors speak any English. If you don't speak fluent Spanish then having a realtor that speaks your language is essential.

Most realtors seem to be old women. Surprisingly, many are not that knowledgeable about the property market in general or what's on their books. Although it doesn't seem to make good business sense many realtors are only really interested in selling you what's on their books - that way they get both the buyer and seller's commission and don't have to share it with another realtor. They will promise to search the market though their databases and to find you the best properties, but frequently they don't. They act in their best interests, not yours.

15. Choosing A Realtor

Some less-than reputable realtors will also not be strictly honest with the sales particulars for the properties on their books. Sizes and lighting levels are frequently inflated, but other details may be misrepresented too. This is covered in further detail in the *Viewing Property* chapter.

There are many realtors out there, all of whom will be only too keen for your business. It is crucial that you find one that you can converse with comfortably in the language of your choice, and that is honest and ethical and who will actually work hard for you and do what they claim.

To not choose the right realtor could be a costly mistake. Ask a potential realtor pertinent questions and use your gut feel. Ask them for a list of clients that can recommend them and make sure that you speak to those clients and verify their claims. Choosing the right realtor is one of the most important decisions to get right. I can't stress this strongly enough.

The supplementary appendix to this book contains details of English-speaking realtors who I've worked with extensively and who are honest and reliable.

16. The Difference Between Realtors & Property Investment Consultants

Put simply, a realtor sells property and a consultant sells advice. However, there are many areas where their services overlap.

Both a consultant and a realtor will help you identify properties, accompany you on viewings and help you make an offer. Both will give some sort of advice on specific properties and the property market in general. But there are differences.

Firstly, a consultant is being paid to be independent, and should offer impartial advice. You are paying for their professional knowledge. At the end of the day it probably doesn't matter to them whether you buy a given property or not, they have no financial interest in it.

A realtor, on the other hand, stands to make a commission from selling you a property (a double commission if it's a property on their books). They have a financial interest in you making that purchase. For that reason, the advice they give you will most likely not be totally impartial, it will be skewed towards encouraging you to make that offer. They may not actually lie, but they may omit to tell you all the facts. Some realtors are worse than others. It is in their interests for you to pay as high a price as possible as they stand to receive a percentage of the selling price. They have no real incentive to help you get a lower price when it means they will make less money.

Never will you hear a realtor say "...well actually, that property is priced too high. I think you should offer so and so..." It just

16. The Difference Between Realtors & Investment Consultants

doesn't happen. A consultant, on the other hand, will offer you that sort of advice. That's part of what you're paying for.

Also, post sale, a realtor will only be able to offer you the most general of advice about refurbishment and other post-sale matters. It isn't part of their business so they simply will not know. I've come across a realtor who couldn't even advise a client where to go to buy a bed for her new apartment - such a matter was beyond the realm of the realtor's experience. A good consultant will know precisely the answers to this sort of question. A good consultant will also know how to go about getting a property renovated, and will have contacts for project managers (if necessary) and reliable tradespeople.

17. Viewing Properties - Factors To Consider

At some point you will be given a property specification sheet - these are discussed in a later chapter.

Unless you are viewing a property you've arranged to view yourself from a newspaper, or are turning up as part of an open day, you will be accompanied by your realtor when viewing properties.

If the buying and selling realtor are different, as is usually the case, then you will also meet the seller's realtor at the property, and it will be he or she that actually shows you and your realtor around. It's also possible that the owner will be there, or other occupiers of the property. Usually, the owner will not mind if you wish to take photographs and the realtors will encourage you to do so for later comparison between properties.

Other factors aside (which are discussed later), I tend to tell people to go with their gut feel. Does the property feel right? Does it have a good vibe? Is the layout good? Or does something repel you about it? This kind of subjective judgement is hard to quantify but you will probably know more or less straight away if it feels right or not (most won't).

Sometimes there can be an awkwardness after you've been shown around a property where the realtors are hoping to convince you to buy it. They may dawdle there unnecessarily. If it doesn't feel right then don't waste your time - say you've seen enough, thank the seller's realtor politely and say it's time to go.

A rule of thumb I personally use is to ask myself: "Could I see myself living here for a few months if I had to?" I know I said earlier

17. Viewing Properties - Factors To Consider

than if you are buying for investment you should use your head, not your heart, but in this case we are looking at the interior of a specific property and not the location. If it feels right for you, chances it will feel right for other people as well, which is important when it comes to renting.

As well as having to feel right, there are other factors to take into account before getting to the stage of even considering making an offer. These are discussed below.

Light

Many apartments can be quite dark inside, with limited natural light. For the locals this may not be much of a problem, particularly if they've grown up living in dark apartments and have never known anything different. From their point of view darkness isn't necessarily a bad thing - in the heat of the summer the small windows which reduce the light will also help keep an apartment cooler as there's less scope for solar warming. In the days before air conditioning this was important.

Whilst the locals don't usually have a problem with lack of light, Europeans and North Americans often consider such apartments to be gloomy inside. Therefore, you ideally want an apartment that has a lot of natural light if these are the people you will be renting to.

Apart from window size, other factors may influence the light levels: e.g. are there other buildings or obstructions nearby that block the light? Which way is north? (Remember in the southern hemisphere, the sunny side is to the north.) If it's an evening

The Complete Guide To Real Estate Investment In Argentina

viewing, or the day is dull, you might want to come back for another look when the light conditions are different.

Most apartment windows have steel or wooden shutters which can be lowered from inside. As well as providing privacy, they can also be used to shut out the heat of the sun. In some locations (e.g. ground floor) they also provide a security element.

Noise

Cities are noisy places. Buenos Aires is no exception with its constant stream of traffic belting around the streets. Add to this the noisy buses that barrel down the avenues and main arteries, the frequent clanging of garbage trucks and the roar from planes at the city airport if the wind is in the right direction and you will see that parts of Buenos Aires can be very noisy at times.

Noise is undesirable, but is inevitable in a city. Obviously a noisy apartment is less desirable than a quieter one. Generally speaking, apartments at street and the lower levels will be subject to most noise - they are also more likely to be subject to pollution (vehicle fumes or smog). Properties located on the busy avenues tend to be the worst - I know one person who lives on the fourth floor on Santa Fe who has to shut her window whilst she's on the phone otherwise she can't hear anything over the traffic roar!

It's worth noting that traffic patterns can vary depending on time of day, and between weekdays and weekends. A quiet apartment viewed on a Saturday afternoon may be extremely noisy come Monday morning. You are well advised to revisit an apartment at different times to check this out. You don't necessarily have to

17. Viewing Properties - Factors To Consider

arrange a viewing each time, often just standing outside the block will be sufficient.

Another noise consideration which is frequently overlooked is elevator noise. The low throb of the motors can often vibrate through a building, particularly with older systems. You will most likely visit an apartment in the daytime when the elevators are quiet, but they will usually be quite busy in the early mornings and early evenings as people go to and from work. Again, you are advised to check back. You don't want to buy an otherwise perfect apartment only to find the peace is impaired by incessant elevator noise at certain times.

Balcony

The majority of apartments will have a balcony of one sort or another. They can be anything from two square metres with a roof overhead that forms the balcony for the floor above, up to something of a reasonable size that is more open that you can fit a table and chairs on. Some bigger apartments may even have two or more balconies.

Sometimes the owner will have boxed in a balcony with glass walls and removed the original door or window leading to it, effectively increasing the area inside the apartment. In this case the balcony will be more like a small conservatory. Usually these conversions have windows which can be opened.

Apartments on the top floor (commonly the eighth) will often have a patio or terrace that is open to the sky, usually a much larger area than most balconies. This is one of the reasons why top floor apartments are desirable.

Ground floor apartments may have a private garden or yard. They tend to be quite dark because of the height of the surrounding buildings and will get little (if any) direct sun - although this may be a blessing in the height of summer. These gardens are also overlooked by all the higher apartments, so afford little privacy.

All balconies and private outdoor areas (e.g. patios) form part of the square metreage recorded in the property title. Whilst having an outdoor area is undoubtedly nice, Argentineans often perceive internal square metreage (i.e. indoors) as providing better value for money, and may prefer a bigger apartment with no terrace over a smaller one with a terrace even though the total area may be the same size.

Personally, I like to live in a place where I have an outside area, so a balcony is essential as a bare minimum. I imagine if you were buying a place to live in you would feel the same. From a rental point of view a balcony or terrace is a big plus point. I would therefore always advise you to buy a property with a least a balcony.

However a balcony isn't just a balcony. The view is important. If it overlooks a wonderful cityscape that is a big plus compared to one from where you can only see the block opposite. Also you need to consider how much natural light it gets and whether it faces the sun. If it does, will it be in the shadow of other buildings? These factors are probably more important if you are buying as your home as opposed for renting.

17. Viewing Properties - Factors To Consider

Sometimes, owners put up strong wire mesh or screens around their balconies. Whilst on the planta baja or first floor this might make sense from a security point of view, often this is done on much higher floors which at first seems a little odd as not all apartments have it. The reason people do it is because they have young children and it allows them to play safely on the balcony without fear that they will climb over the railing and fall.

These safety screens are ugly and make a balcony look like part of a prison. Personally I find them rather claustrophobic. Unless you have young children I would always recommend removing them as they have a detrimental effect on the visual appearance of a property.

Occasionally you may come across an apartment block that appears to stand on concrete columns, like stilts. The ground floor is little more than a paved area open to the weather. In this case the ground floor is a communal area where residents can hold barbecues and parties. This type of apartment block is more common outside of central Buenos Aires - probably not somewhere where tourists would stay.

Bathroom Facilities

Some studios and smaller apartments may only have a shower and a tiny bathroom. Personally I think it's important that a place has a full bathroom with a hot tub.

If you were going to be living in the place yourself would you like just a shower? Probably not. Equally, if you are going to be renting the place out you're going to be competing with hotels that provide full bathroom facilities. Not having one puts you at a disadvantage. Even though most people probably won't use the hot tub they still like to have it there.

Note that the hot tub doesn't necessarily have to be full size; the smaller ¾ size tubs (1.40m) which are quite common are perfectly acceptable.

Flooring

The majority of apartments are built with wooden parquet floors, which can look stunning. Many Argentineans consider fitted carpets dirty and unhygienic.

Most rental agents will tell you that tenants prefer a wooden floor to carpet, and that it will make the place easier to rent to both locals and tourists. I agree with this.

If an apartment has carpets, pull back a corner to see if there is a wooden floor underneath. Often, carpets are just laid over parquet. If underneath you find concrete then you may want to re-evaluate the suitability of this apartment.

Don't worry if the carpet has been glued onto the wood, or if an uncarpeted floor is in a dirty or dingy condition. It is an inexpensive process to get the floor professionally sanded and re-lacquered (*plastificado*), making it as good as new. The price for restoring a floor is about US$12 per square metre.

17. Viewing Properties - Factors To Consider

Gym, Pool, Laundry, Sauna And Other Facilities

These kind of facilities are more common in newer buildings. If the place is for you yourself to live in then their presence or absence is a matter or personal choice.

If the place is to rent out to tourists then facilities such as these could be important if you are going for the luxury end of the market. In this case you will be competing with upscale hotels that have these facilities. Even though most people will never use them they still like to have them.

The cost of providing these services is included in the monthly expenses. Often, the facilities themselves may not be that good and maybe designed more for show (the snob factor). I've seen small pools that aren't really big enough to swim in and gyms that are little more than a couple of weight machines in a room. Probably only one or two people in the whole block will ever actually use them.

Many consultants will tell you that having such facilities is essential for the rental market. In some circumstances that may be true. I take the view that you need to look at them from a return on investment perspective. You need to try to ascertain how much more the property you are looking at costs because it has these facilities (by comparison with similar properties located close by without them). Next you need to look at the expensas to work out how much they cost each month to run. Taking these factors into consideration you need to decide if you will get value from paying this extra - i.e. will it bring in more revenue than it costs.

It's not always easy to quantify the figures. Often you have to rely on a gut feel for if it's right or not. Here again a good consultant should be able to advise you.

Don't take the presence or not of these facilities in isolation - consider them in the context of the whole apartment.

Air conditioning

Most consultants will tell you that air conditioning is essential for the rental market. They are right, especially in the summer.

My own view it that is nice to have air conditioning in an apartment you are buying, but not essential. This is because it is very easy and straightforward to fit later.

Air conditioning comes in many forms, but the most common is known as a split. A split is a 2-part unit - a fan box which goes outside on an exterior wall to dispose of excess heat, which is connected to an interior unit that blows the cold air into the room and is adjusted with a remote control. The better models are reversible which means they can also suck heat out of the atmosphere and blow warm air into the apartment in winter.

Split units start from upwards of US$350 and cost in the region of US$120 to install. It is therefore relatively inexpensive to fit air conditioning in an apartment that doesn't have it.

One thing to bear in mind is the condition of the windows. If the frames are old and rusty and don't fit tightly then this is obviously going to impinge on the efficiency of any air conditioning.

17. Viewing Properties - Factors To Consider

Garage Facility

Some buildings include designated parking bays at street or basement levels in a communal garage. The bay(s) designated for each apartment form part of the title to the property. Having a garage will obviously add to the price of an apartment.

For the short-term rental market, having a garage probably isn't important. Most tourists staying in Buenos Aires won't have a car. Even if they do, on-street parking generally isn't problematic (although like everywhere the number of vehicles on the road is increasing so parking is becoming harder).

For upscale long-term rentals having a garage space is important when the rent is in excess of US$900 per month.

Centralized (Communal) Hot Water And Heating

Many apartment blocks have centralized hot water. Basically, water is heated by a giant boiler that is normally located in the basement of the building. Hot water is piped to each apartment and is usually available on a 24 hour basis. The cost is shared amongst the tenants and paid for via the monthly expensas.

In some buildings where the hot water is communal, centralized heating is provided as well. The boiler powers a separate radiator circuit which runs through each apartment and feeds the radiators. Usually, radiators have individual control valves to allow some independent regulation of the temperature. The heating will be switched on and off by the building's caretaker as he thinks appropriate. Typically, the heating will only be used for three or perhaps four months of the year. Depending on the temperature it may only be switched on at certain times of the day - e.g. early morning.

From a rental perspective there is no distinct advantage or disadvantage to having centralized hot water and/or heating. From an economic point of view it probably costs about the same as each apartment providing its own heating.

Baulera

A baulera is an additional storage area located in the basement that belongs to an apartment. It is effectively a large, lockable cupboard. Typically they are about two square metres of floor area and of ceiling height. Locals tend to use them for long-term storage for things that aren't needed very often, such as tins of paint or winter clothes put away for summer.

Usually there is no direct access to the bauleras, and it will be necessary to ask the caretaker to unlock the basement so that you can go down.

If you are living in a place yourself a baulera can undoubtedly be useful. From a rental point of view it adds no value at all as most tenants won't even know it's there, and even if they did the logistics of gaining access to it means that using it isn't practical.

Many landlords use their baulera to keep their personal property in.

Price

This is probably the biggest factor of all. There is no general price guide as to what is a fair and reasonable price. The asking price

17. Viewing Properties - Factors To Consider

can vary widely for similar apartments in the same building by tens of thousands of dollars. For reasons already discussed, at no point will a realtor tell you that something is overpriced.

The price per square metre for a given area (see previous chapters) should be taken as a rough guide only, and you should account for inflation since the book was published (updated figures are provided in the supplementary appendix). Factors such as the actual location (e.g. quiet side street), floor level and general condition will all play their part on the price. At the end of the day the old adage is true: something is only worth what someone is prepared to pay for it.

By viewing properties in an area you will begin to get a feel for what the going rate is in that neighborhood, and with time will begin to know when something is fairly priced. Remember no official comparison data is available and 80% of the time property transactions are recorded at well below the real selling price. Of course a good consultant will be able to help you here, and the potential savings could more than cover their fees.

In the end, whether an apartment is worth a certain amount has to come down to a subjective judgment from you, taking all the above factors into consideration. You need to consider the return on investment, as discussed in an earlier chapter.

Don't forget that the asking price will almost certainly not be price that you would offer.

The Complete Guide To Real Estate Investment In Argentina

18. The Property Specification Sheet

For each apartment that you view you will be given a property specification sheet. Ideally you will have this before your visit, but frequently it will be handed to you by the seller's realtor when you arrive.

Sometimes the spec sheet is more of a sales brochure and may include photographs of the property and possibly a floor plan. Other times it might just be a specification list on a piece of paper.

The spec sheet contains the property address, floor level, monthly expenses, whether a telephone line is present, likewise cable TV and other general factors including the realtor's commission. The information will most likely be in Spanish (unless the realtor is marketing to foreigners) and may use similar abbreviations to those explained in the newspaper advertisements section.

The spec should contain a luminosity scale. This is a number between one and ten that measures the amount of natural light. However, the light level is a subjective matter and it's very common for the selling realtor's opinion of what is a high light level to be very different from most people's. Apartments are frequently recorded as having a high light level when in my opinion they don't. Sometimes a subjective adjective is used rather than an absolute figure - e.g. Light level: High.

The spec will also state the number of square metres the apartment comprises. Often this is incorrect, and the size will have been overstated by the selling realtor. At first it's very hard to equate a number (e.g. 70 square metres) to how big an actual

18. The Property Specification Sheet

apartment is going to be, particularly if it is odd-shaped. However, with time you will begin to get a feel for what a certain size should encompass, and you should be able to guesstimate fairly accurately the size of an apartment when you see it. Since property is priced more or less by the square metre it's very important that you have an accurate size.

Overstating the size is common and I've come to the conclusion that sometimes overstating is done deliberately by the selling realtor to make the property sound more attractive; at other times the realtor may just have taken the seller's word for it; and sometimes they just don't have a clue what size something is and just put what they think it should be.

Many consultants suggest that you take a tape measure and physically measure up. This isn't as easy as it sounds, as things like internal walls have to be taken into consideration; the square metreage includes everything inside an apartment and isn't just the sum of the room dimensions. Built in cupboards and wardrobes, balconies and other irregular spaces all have to be included.

Personally, I don't recommend that you waste time with a tape measure. There's a much easier way to find out the true size - it's recorded on the title to the property. In an ideal world the seller's realtor will have a copy of the property title - if not, the seller should be able to supply them with one. You should ask your realtor to demand to see a copy of the front page. If the seller is serious about selling, they will get this for you.

When a wrong size is identified and pointed out, there's never an apology from the selling realtor. You will usually get excuses like

The Complete Guide To Real Estate Investment In Argentina

it's a printing mistake. They don't seem unduly bothered by being caught out - it's just part of doing business here.

The best thing to do with specification sheets is to treat them as a rough guide only. Don't take everything they say at face value. Check the stated facts out for yourself. The old adage "buyer beware" is as true today as it ever was.

Note that property is sold "ad corpus"; a Latin phrase which in this context means that you buy what you see. This will be stated in the purchase agreement.

19. How Many Times To See a Place Before Making An Offer

This is a common question and there's no right or wrong answer. It depends entirely on you.

I know people who have made an offer on an apartment after only seeing it once. It felt right to them and they were happy to proceed. On the other hand some people like to go back two, three or four times to make certain it really does have what they want. If everything feels right but you are unsure, if possible I suggest that you take along someone else to get a second opinion. You may be caught up in the emotion of wanting to buy somewhere but a friend may be more objective.

Don't forget that it's a good idea to go back at different times on different days to check out light and noise levels, which may be different from your first viewing.

If a property still feels right after you've paid consideration to all the above factors, then you should consider making an offer. This is discussed in the next chapter.

20. Making An Offer

The Offer Process:

When you make an offer, you have to put down a reservation fee to show that you are serious. Typically this will be 3% - 5% of the offer, but there's no hard and fast rule as to the amount. I've know people who have been asked to put down as little as 1,000 pesos, and as much as US$10,000, although the amount asked tends to be a reflection of the value of the property. US$2,000 is quite a common figure. This reservation fee is known as a *reserva* and it's held in trust by the realtor.

By paying the reserva you are effectively blocking the apartment for the offer period, and the selling realtor cannot show it during this time. The offer period is usually a week and is specified as part of your offer. The seller has to respond by the deadline. If they fail to (not that I've ever known this to happen) then you get the reserva back.

During the offer period the seller can accept, reject, or counteroffer. Usually they will counteroffer, and there will follow a period of haggling, as you may counteroffer their counteroffer, which in turn may be counteroffered, and so on. It's basically the same process of negotiating a real estate deal that you would experience in Europe or North America.

If the seller rejects the offer, or a price cannot be agreed following a counteroffer, then the reserva will be returned to you and the selling realtor will be free to start showing the property again.

20. Making An Offer

Where the parties agree on a price, the reserva will be deducted from the balance of the commission owed to the realtor.

If an offer is genuinely low, then the selling realtor may refuse to transmit it to the seller. This is accepted practice.

Sometimes an unscrupulous realtor will refuse to pass on an offer when it's reasonable, claiming that it's too low. They are hoping to trap you into making a higher offer which will earn them more commission. If this happens you may have to be quite insistent with them. If possible, try to speak to the seller directly - it's not uncommon for a seller to sack their realtor once they've been made aware of their sharp practices.

Another common trick is for a realtor not to pass on a seller's acceptance of an offer. They may claim the offer has been rejected, thus inviting a higher offer from the buyer which again will earn them more commission. If the buyer refuses they can always say the seller has changed their mind and now wants to accept.

If possible, you should always try to speak directly to the seller if an offer has been rejected. Things may not be as they seem and the seller may be very surprised to hear what you've been told. Buyers are discouraged by the realtors from talking directly to the seller, but you've been to their property so you know where they live, or else someone living there will know. Go back and ask.

If an offer has genuinely been rejected then talking directly to be seller can often shed light on why. It usually easier to agree on a price by talking than going through a formal series of offers and counteroffers.

The mentality of some realtors seems to be not to lose a penny in commission and they would sometimes rather let a deal fall through than earn a lesser amount. It's illogical, but that's how some of them think.

Another thing to bear in mind is that some of the more unethical realtors may continue to try to sell the property during the period of the reserva, even though they are not supposed to. It's possible to find out by getting someone to phone them up to arrange a viewing, although there's not really very much you can do about it - apart from giving them a very strong piece of your mind of course.

Deciding How Much To Offer:
Naturally sellers want to get the maximum price they can for their property and naturally a buyer wants to pay the minimum possible. Hopefully, somewhere between these competing forces a deal can be struck.

It's almost a given rule that when putting a property on the market a seller will overprice it, so that there is some room to negotiate to reach the price they will accept (or higher). An apartment that a seller thinks is worth US$120,000 may be put on the market for US$130,000, for example.

Likewise, a buyer will almost always offer less initially than they are prepared to pay, so they too have negotiating room.

So, how do you go about deciding how much to offer? It's a good question, but there isn't an exact answer, only some general guidelines. At the end of the day the decision is yours (although a

20. Making An Offer

good consultant can advise you of what's reasonable in the particular circumstances).

As I've said before, there isn't an index of what constitutes a fair and reasonable price. Firstly, try to establish what you think the value of the property is based on your experience of seeing similar properties in the area. (If your figure is higher than the asking price then something's very wrong!)

Next, work out as accurately as you can the return on investment assuming that purchase price. Does it give an acceptable rate of return? If it does, then I suggest you use this figure (or thereabouts) as your maximum purchase price. Hopefully, this figure will be in the same general ballpark as the asking price - if not see below.

If the ROI isn't acceptable, work it out again several times using a slightly lower figure each time. By a bit of trial and error you should come up with a purchase price that gives you an acceptable ROI. If this is still reasonably close to the asking price then all well and good - if not see below.

Now you have the maximum price that you are prepared to pay. For the reasons already indicated you don't want to offer this amount straightaway. If your maximum price is close to the asking price then as a rule of thumb I would consider offering between 90 and 95% of the asking price. Any less could be considered insulting.

If your maximum price is considerably lower than the asking price the situation is more problematic. It's most likely that either your assumptions are incorrect (so double-check everything) or the

95

property is considerably overpriced. You may want to offer what you consider a reasonable amount, but remember that realtors can refuse to transmit an offer that they consider too low, so be prepared for rejection. However, sometimes sellers try it on just to see what they can get (stories of rich foreigners paying considerably over the odds abound), so all may not be lost. But if you and the seller can't even get in the same ballpark, then I suggest you walk away and carry on looking at other properties.

I stress again - the price to offer is a subjective figure that can only be decided by you, bearing in mind all the particular circumstances relating to a particular property.

Most likely, once you've made your offer, the seller will come back with a counteroffer. You need to consider if you are happy to accept the counteroffer, and if not to come back with another counteroffer of your own. This process may happen a few times. Make sure that you don't get carried away in the heat of the moment and offer more than your maximum price, or accept a counteroffer more than your maximum price.

Again, the figure to accept in a counteroffer is a subjective figure that can only be decided by you, bearing in mind all the particular circumstances relating to a particular property. If you are happy to buy at that price, then go ahead and accept it. Congratulations - you've now agreed on the purchase price.

The above points are only general guidelines. You might like to also take into consideration how desperate the seller is to sell - as a simple rule of thumb the more desperate the seller is the more likely they are to accept a lower offer.

20. Making An Offer

It won't always be easy to determine the seller's situation, but there are sometimes a few clues. You need to take note of all the little details. The length of time a property has been on the market is often important. (Sales particulars may contain they date they were prepared, which can be a giveaway.) Other factors could include the seller having young children and wanting to move to somewhere bigger, the seller wanting to move into a retirement home, or executors trying to dispose of a property under a will. There may be countless other reasons why a seller could be keen to sell - the key is to try to discover them.

Bear in mind that if a property represents good value and has generated a lot of interest, the seller may not negotiate at all.

(Sometimes a seller may insist as a condition of the sale that the sale is officially recorded as being for a lower price. This is for tax reasons. A discussion of this topic can be found in the Escritura section - for now you need to know that it's probably not a good idea.)

Stamp Tax

In Buenos Aires stamp tax is waived for the first property bought, provided the value is under US$120,000. This exemption does <u>not</u> apply to foreigners, who will have to pay the tax at 2.5% of the sale price, as will a buyer who already owns a property. Sometimes the tax is split 50:50 between buyer and seller, although usually the seller will often insist that the buyer pays it as a condition of the sale. The buyer must ask for it to be split at the time of making the offer, as you can guarantee the seller won't agree to split it later.

21. Building Surveys

In Europe and the US it is common for a buyer to have a survey done before a real estate purchase is finalized in order to ensure there is nothing fundamentally wrong with the property. The survey will indicate the current market value and confirm that the buyer is paying a fair price. Usually these surveys are instigated on behalf of mortgage companies to ensure that their loan capital is sufficiently protected if they need to repossess the property.

In Argentina, as a foreigner you won't be purchasing with a mortgage, so there's no requirement to have a survey to satisfy a third party. The decision to commission a survey is entirely yours. Bear in mind that there isn't an index of current prices or the concept of what is a fair price, so any survey you commission will only comment on the condition of the property, not the value.

The vast majority of buyers (both local and foreign) do not commission a survey, especially if they are buying an apartment. The administrator has a legal duty to maintain the building so you can be pretty sure it will be in a reasonable condition. Also, by law the building has to be insured so in the unlikely event of an unforeseen problem (e.g. subsidence) the building will be covered. However, always use common sense - you can get a pretty good idea of the condition of a building and whether it has been well maintained just by looking at it.

If you do decide to commission a survey your realtor should be able to recommend a qualified surveyor - usually an architect that will produce a report for US$100 - US$350 depending on the type and size of the property.

23. Once The Offer Is Agreed: Boletos, Senas and Escrituras

22. Escribanos - What They Do And How To Choose One

Part of the reason that the system of property title registration works well in Argentina is because every transaction must go through a *notario publico* (authorized notary) and a central office that documents every single buy and sell.

An *escribano* is a lawyer qualified to deal with property transactions, who has undergone an additional two years of university training. Escribanos are qualified notaries and will notarize the relevant forms and documents relating to the property purchase. In the UK they would be called a conveyencing solicitor, and in the US a real-estate attorney.

In essence, the escribano will study the property title, verify the ownership rights of the seller and the transmission of the property rights for the last ten years. He will ensure there aren't any liens, mortgages, warrants or anything else affecting the rights of the property the seller is selling. If there are, he will make ensure they are paid off by the seller so that it passes free of encumbrance on the date of sale. (In the unlikely event that this can't be achieved, he will inform you of the position and you can either walk away from the deal or renegotiate the price. In practice, I've never known this to happen.)

In practice the buyer has the right to choose the escribano, not the seller. This makes perfect sense - you will be the party paying the escribano so they will be acting on your behalf to ensure the title is valid and free of encumbrance and correctly registered in your name. If you are buying a new development the construction firm can insist that you use their escribano. This is for technical reasons to do with the fact that the escribano will be organizing many new titles. If it isn't a new construction, always insist on appointing your own escribano.

Escribanos normally charge a flat fee that is a percentage of the sale price. This usually ranges from 1.5% up to about 4%, depending on the individual escribano. It will be subject to VAT. Paying a higher fee doesn't necessarily get you a better service. The quality of the escribano is paramount, not the cost. Finding an honest and reliable escribano is essential.

Generally, you can be reasonably sure that an escribano will do a fair job with respect to verification of the property title and correctly registering it into your name. This is because they are qualified professionals and if they didn't do their job properly they could be sued by you for negligence, which could lead to them being struck off. However, this doesn't mean that all escribanos are good - there are many tricks and scams the more unscrupulous will use to try to coax more money out of you. Sometimes this may not be deliberate, they may be unclear on revisions to the law or just simply not know how to apply them properly.

The most common is charging the buyer a phantom stamp tax. Stamp tax (covered in a later section) is a tax levied by local government at 2.5% of the purchase price. There are exemptions for first-time buyers, however recent changes in the law mean foreigners do not now qualify for these. Whilst escribanos can no longer add this tax and pocket it themselves, they have been known to add a higher rate than that officially in force.

23. Once The Offer Is Agreed: Boletos, Senas and Escrituras

Escribanos only get paid their fee when you close on a property and hand over the cash to the seller. This can provide a motive for unethical escribanos to push through deals that really shouldn't go through.

Some of the cheaper escribanos may bill you extra amounts for things like registration and title fees, along with other disbursements. The better escribanos will include these in their percentage fee and won't charge for them individually. It is therefore extremely important to establish exactly what is and what isn't included in the standard fee.

It's a legal requirement that if a foreign national does not speak a good level of Spanish then at the point of completion a registered legal translator has to be present to translate the legal papers and title document into a language that the buyer understands. This process has to be witnessed and notarized on record and is to prove the buyer fully understands the nature and detail of the transaction. Again, if you will need a translator you need to be clear if this will be included in the escribano's fee or if you will be charged additionally.

It is more than likely that your realtor will try to recommend an escribano. This doesn't necessarily mean that they are any good. The realtor may well receive a commission or backhander, and so have their own interests at heart, not yours. In the very worst cases realtors and escribanos have been known to conspire to deliberately mislead naive buyers into paying false taxes and other costs which they then share amongst themselves.

The Complete Guide To Real Estate Investment In Argentina

Whilst all will speak Spanish, the number of escribanos that speak English to a good standard is not high. As with choosing your realtor, choosing an escribano that you can communicate with is of paramount importance.

Using a good escribano who is ethical and understands the law fully can save you thousands of dollars. The lowest quoted fees may be a false economy. When deciding on an escribano the same general advice about choosing a realtor applies - use your gut feel and check out recommendations from former clients. Again, a good consultant (if you are using one) should be able to help - although you should make sure they recommend several escribanos to reduce the chance of collusion and sharp practice.

The supplementary appendix to this book contains details of good English-speaking escribanos who are known to be ethical, reliable and honest, along with their current fees.

Since July 2007 escribanos have had to notify all property transactions to AFIP (*Control sobre la documentación de respaldo* - Endorsement control). If there is more than a 20% discrepancy between what AFIP believe the true value is according to their actuarial tables and the reported value they may investigate further. The recorded value will also be taken into consideration with respect to asset tax declarations.

23. What Happens Once The Offer Is Agreed: Boletos, Senas and Escrituras

Once the purchase price has been agreed, there are basically two different ways to proceed - *boletos* and *senas*. Which option is best depends on how quickly the sale can be completed.

Boleto de compraventa:

A boleto de compraventa (commonly called a boleto) is effectively a contract between the buyer and seller. The seller obligates himself to transfer the property to the buyer on a given date, and the buyer agrees to pay for the property on that date. The boleto regulates the conditions of the sale and will have clauses allowing the sale to be forfeit if the escribano finds anything untoward with the title.

Taking the boleto route you effectively make a down payment to the seller - usually 30%, but the exact figure is negotiable. I recommend putting down at least 25% because if the seller goes bankrupt you will have priority under the law. The boleto is basically the point of no return for both buyer and seller and is more or less analogous to exchanging contracts in the UK.

If the seller backs out or fails to transfer the property on the given date, by law he has to return double the down payment to the buyer - double as half is the return of the buyer's original payment, the other half an equal penalty payment for breaking the contract. Likewise, if the buyer fails to honour the contract he forfeits the down payment and the seller keeps it. As an alternative to keeping the payment the injured party has the legal right to enforce the deal. These apparently harsh penalties are designed to stop gazumping.

A boleto would typically be used where there is likely to be a reasonably long time before the sale will actually take place. Typical reasons could include the seller needing time to move out, or because a new building hasn't yet been completed.

The deal can collapse anytime up to the point the boleto is notarized by both parties - the boleto locks them in. Sometimes a seller will back out of signing the boleto at the last minute in an attempt to get more money. If this happens there's not much you can do. Sometimes the seller will be only too keen to sign if he sees that you are not going be blackmailed into paying more and are prepared to walk away from the deal.

All realtors' fees are paid at the time of the boleto. The seller takes possession of the down payment and the date is set for the title deed transfer, known as the escritura. The escribano who will be handling the purchase is also specified. (The escribano is paid at the time of the escritura.)

The boleto contract is usually standard, although several variants exist to reflect differing circumstances, for example if the building is still under construction.

For your protection you should have the boleto contract checked by a qualified lawyer or your escribano.

Sena

The other option after the purchase price has been agreed is to go straight to the escritura, with the intention of completing on the

23. Once The Offer Is Agreed: Boletos, Senas and Escrituras

transaction as quickly as possible. In this case the realtors' fees will be paid at the time of the escritura (a notional boleto is considered to be signed at that time).

There are significant risks in going straight to the escritura. No formal contract exists between buyer and seller until the escritura, so until then the seller is free to walk away from the deal without paying any compensation. If this happens you are likely to have incurred legal or other costs which you can't recover.

However, it is possible to mitigate these risks by use of a *sena*. A sena is a private contract between the buyer and seller that works in a similar way to a boleto. It locks in both parties. Typically with the sena the buyer would put down about US$10,000, but the amount is negotiable with the seller. If either party breaks the contract the rules are essentially the same as with a boleto - the buyer loses his payment, and the seller has to pay back double.

If you are going straight to escritura I would always recommend using a sena for your own protection. The realtors might try to talk you into doing a boleto instead - this is so they get their commission as soon as possible. Don't listen to them, unless there is a valid reason for doing a boleto. Once the sena is in place your realtor should help keep things on track as they have their commission incentive.

Again, for your protection you should have the sena contract checked by a qualified lawyer or your escribano.

The key difference between a sena and a boleto is that with a sena either party can get out of the deal by paying the penalty, whereas with a boleto the injured party optionally has the right to enforce the deal instead. Therefore, boletos provide a higher rate of certainty that a purchase will go through.

Escritura

The act of taking possession of a property is formalized in an *escritura* by a notary. After the escritura has been signed by all parties the escribano will carry out the formalities of registering the buyer's details in the public property register.

The escritura document itself initially identifies the seller by means of name, ID number, date of birth, tax number, address and the names of both parents. It is quite bureaucratic, but that's the way people are legally identified in Argentina.

Similar details are recorded about the buyer. If you are not a national or don't have residency status in Argentina then your ID number will be your passport number. Your tax number is covered in a later section - basically you can't buy property without it.

The escritura will then describe the property in detail - the precise location, block number, street, nearest cross street and what zone it's in. The total square metreage of the property title is listed, along with the percentage of the total building the apartment occupies and details of the building management association.

The escritura may also describe the phone number of the telephone line associated with the property (see under Utilities later).

Next is a section in which the notary certifies that following his investigations into the title and the certificates he has obtained, the

23. Once The Offer Is Agreed: Boletos, Senas and Escrituras

seller has no legal restrictions on transferring the property and that it is free from warrants, liens and mortgages.

In the final section the escribano certifies the purchase price and that he has witnessed that the buyer has paid it to the seller in his presence. The seller agrees to acquit himself of all rights over the property and transfer them to the buyer. The buyer accepts this transfer to become the new owner.

All parties sign the escritura and the purchase is legally complete. The escribano should give the buyer a notarized copy of the property title.

If you are not an Argentinean national and don't speak fluent Spanish then it's a legal requirement that a qualified legal translator is present to translate the documents into a language you understand. This has to be witnessed and notarized on record and is to prove the buyer fully understands the nature and detail of the transaction.

At the escritura meeting the seller should give you a copy of the building's rules and regulations. These stipulate the rules that an apartment owner is bound by (e.g. use of property for business purposes, noise restrictions, etc) and describe how the building is to be run and the process for conflict resolution. Essentially, these are formalized common sense and are pretty standard across all buildings. If the seller doesn't have a copy of the rules you should be able to get one from the management association.

At the escritura meeting the seller will provide proof to the esribano that the service and local tax bills have been paid to date. Services are usually attached to the property rather than the owner

The Complete Guide To Real Estate Investment In Argentina

so it's important to establish that there are no bills outstanding which you would become liable for as the new owner. Usually the seller may not be able to prove that all current bills have been paid (e.g. if a bill is only issued bimonthly), so in this case the escribano will hold (say) a hundred dollars of the seller's money, to be paid over once proof of payment is received.

If the buyer receives a bill relating to the period before purchase, he should forward it to the escribano and it will be deducted from the funds held. Bills that cover a dual period of ownership are worked out on a pro-rata basis.

As stated several times, almost all property purchases in Argentina are in cash. The buyer will have with him thousands of dollars in hundred dollar bills (getting hold of the cash and safety issues are discussed in detail later). They will be counted out in front of everyone and given to the seller. In fact they will probably be double or triple counted.

The amount paid may be considerably more than the amount recorded in the escritura document. Underreporting of a sale price is extremely common in Argentina. This is so the seller will pay less taxes. I've heard of cases where the price has been underreported by as much as 40%.

Usually the seller will request that the price is recorded lower when the offer is accepted, but they have been known to ask later - even once a boleto or sena has been signed.

Although it is illegal, it's a long-established part of the culture in Argentina. It's an example of corruption at the lowest level. The realtors and even the escribano (a qualified professional) don't bat

23. Once The Offer Is Agreed: Boletos, Senas and Escrituras

an eyelid. They turn a blind eye that only sees the transfer of funds up to the recorded amount.

Note that since 2008, when the revised COTI regulations came into effect, sellers now have to get a permit from AFIP before they can put their property up for sale. The permit states the price the seller wishes to put the property on the market for, and if the reported sale price is markedly different then AFIP will investigate the transaction. This has significantly reduced (but not completely eliminated) the scope for under-reporting of the sale price, which is now much less common.

I recommend that you don't take part in such fraud and always insist that the recorded price is the real purchase price. The seller won't like this as it means they will have to pay more taxes, and in some cases they may threaten to pull out of the deal. If this happens there's not much you can do, although often they will accept the fact if they can see your position isn't going to budge. Rarely does the issue of false recording become a showstopper.

There is no benefit to you personally from taking part in this fraud. If you do it could potentially cause you problems later on when you come to sell.

If you haven't gone down the boleto route then both your realtor and the seller's will be at the escritura meeting. It is at this point that they get paid, as does the escribano. All payments are in cash of course, although you should be given receipts.

Note that in Argentina, as in many countries, it is customary practice for the seller to remove most or all light fixtures from a property before a buyer takes possession.

24. Things To Organize Before The Escritura

There are several pieces of "project infrastructure" that have to be in place before the escritura can be completed - namely your tax ID (CDI) and your purchase funds:

Obtaining a CDI Number

It is essential to have an Argentinean tax ID (CDI), otherwise you cannot sign the escritura. The CDI is the equivalent of a Social Security number in the US. CDI stands for *Clave de Identificación* (Identification Key).

The CDI is obtained from the Argentine Federal Tax Agency - the AFIP. The process is relatively simple but it can involve a lot of tedious waiting around.

The first thing you have to do is to obtain an address certificate (*Certificado de Domicilio*) which is issued by the police. To get one you need to go to the local police station that serves the area where you are staying. You will pay a nominal fee, equivalent to a few dollars. The next morning the police will visit your hotel or apartment to confirm that you are staying there, before issuing the certificate. You can be hanging around for hours waiting for them to call.

Once you have the address certificate, you need to visit the AFIP office that serves that address. You need to take two photocopies of your passport with you.

It's unlikely that anyone in the tax office will speak English. Once there you should obtain a CDI application form, which needs filling-in in duplicate. In most AFIP offices you take a number from a

24. Things To Organize Before The Escritura

roll, like at a supermarket deli counter, and wait for that number to be called. Usually you can be hanging around for hours. When it is your turn to go to the desk, hand over the completed forms, your passport, passport copies and the address certificate. If everything is in order they will issue you with a CDI number then and there. The number will be written in the relevant box on one of the copies of the form, which will be officially stamped and handed back to you. You are now a registered Argentinean tax payer and can buy property in Argentina.

There is however a much easier way of getting your CDI. You can let your escribano obtain it for you. Escribanos that deal with foreigner buyers on a regular basis will often include the cost of obtaining a CDI in their quoted fee. If they don't, this can normally be arranged for a fee of less than US$60.

For the escribano to obtain your CDI you will need to sign a Power of Attorney document giving the escribano authority to act on your behalf in this matter. The PoA is basically a standard form, but with typical Argentinean bureaucracy you will have to fill in the details of both your parents. Once the escribano has the Power of Attorney he will send one of his minions off to stand in line for you.

When obtaining a CDI through an escribano, it won't be necessary for the police to visit you, as being a notary the escribano will notarize that your address is correct. Your actual address is irrelevant and is more of an academic point needed to satisfy the bureaucracy of the system.

I strongly recommend that you obtain a CDI through your escribano, as it is far easier.

The Complete Guide To Real Estate Investment In Argentina

Getting The Purchase Cash Into Argentina:

Property purchases in Argentina are currently almost always in cash. Not only is this because the locals don't trust the banks, it also makes it far easier to underreport the purchase price, and is far less traceable. Not only are purchases in cash, but they are in US dollars, which isn't the local currency.

The tax office (AFIP) is pushing for the law to be changed to outlaw cash transactions for real estate purchases. This is to reduce tax evasion caused by false reporting of sale price (which is very easy to do with a cash purchase) and therefore increase tax revenue. Such a change would also help reduce money laundering.

The proposal is that all fund transfers for real estate transactions will have to be notarized, and will have to be made by check (cheque), bank wire/transfer or other financial instrument. Because the payments would be notarized (certified by the escribano as being for the purchase) and traceable, the false reporting of sale price would be made far more difficult.

The government has indicated a willingness to change the law in line with the tax office's proposal, but it is not clear at this stage if such a change in the law will actually be implemented. (A lot of politicians own considerable amounts of property, and whilst they may publicly say they support the change I have it on good authority that in reality many do not want to see a change that could harm their personal interests.) Talk of changing the law has been rumbling on for the last few years, but in the meantime cash remains king.

24. Things To Organize Before The Escritura

Getting hold of physical dollars in Argentina can be one of the most complicated parts of whole property buying process. Short of physically bringing cash with you when you come into the country, which isn't recommended (see below), there will be a cost involved. At a minimum this will add a few percentage points to the total cost of buying the property. The relative merits of the different methods are discussed below.

Official Banks:

If you have an Argentinean bank account you can have funds wired into it from abroad. However, opening an account is not easy, especially if you don't already own property in Argentina or are not a resident. (Opening a bank account is covered in a later chapter.)

Alternatively, maybe you know a trusted local with a bank account who would be happy to receive the funds for you. However, are you really sure you can trust them where large sums of money are involved? Sometimes realtors or consultants will offer to let you use their banking facilities - I would be very dubious about this - what recourse do you have if you don't get all your money?

It's possible that your own bank will have branches in Argentina. The big players like HSBC, Bank Boston and Citibank do. Or maybe your bank has an affiliation (working relationship) with a bank that has. Ask them. Depending on your bank it may be possible to wire funds directly to an affiliated branch in Argentina for your collection.

The Complete Guide To Real Estate Investment In Argentina

Using an official bank to get money into the country is relatively expensive, although the costs have fallen recently. Your funds will be automatically converted from the sending currency into pesos on arrival. The bank will make a few cents on the spread as is always the case with foreign exchange transactions. Typically the forex costs will come to between 1 – 1.5% of the value of the funds transferred.

However, you need US dollars to complete your purchase, not pesos. Your pesos therefore have to undergo a second forex transaction. And guess what - you will be charged a similar amount again, bringing the total cost of bringing dollars into the country to between 2 – 3%.

Even if the original currency that you transferred was US dollars, you will still have to pay these charges to receive it as US dollars in Argentina. Using the official banking system is expensive.

As a result of the government's drive to discourage the use of exchange houses (see next section), pressure has been put on the central bank to reduce foreign exchange charges and exchange rates are now much more competitive than they were. (Using an official bank cost around 3% in 2010). It's probably true to say now that the cost of bringing money in through the official banks is more or less on a par with using a private bank.

Note that for reasons related to retaining capital in the country, (and preventing speculation on the peso), banks are required to withhold 30% of funds wired into Argentina for one year before releasing them to the recipient. This requirement is waived where the funds are being used to purchase a property, however it will be

24. Things To Organize Before The Escritura

necessary to prove to the bank that this is the case by providing the relevant documentation - e.g. a copy of the boleto or sena.

It is still almost impossible to transfer funds through the official banking system within a decent period of time. Be prepared for delays and an awful lot of paperwork.

Exchange Bureaus (Private Banks)

Also known as *casas de cambio* (exchange houses). The way this kind of business works is simple. Basically, you transfer funds in dollars into a bank account outside of Argentina (usually in the US or Europe) that belongs to the exchange bureau. Once the funds have cleared, the exchange bureau will give you the equivalent amount of dollars in cash in Argentina, less their commission of course. Commissions are usually in the 2 - 2.5% ballpark.

Technically you haven't actually transferred funds into Argentina, although the net effect is the same. The government doesn't approve of these pseudo-transfers as they see them as not being beneficial for the economy, amongst other reasons, and has recently ruled using them to be illegal.

Although now technically illegal, a great number of local people use these bureaus. The transfer process is reversible - many Argentineans use their services to transfer their wealth out of Argentina and into foreign bank accounts.

Since 2008 all exchange houses will ask you to prove where the funds come from - as will the official banks - to certify that you are not laundering money (some firms are "loose" divisions of overseas banks, and may have to comply with money laundering legislation in their home country, e.g. The States). You will also be asked to sign a form declaring that the funds are not being laundered. Also, you will have to prove your identify and/or address by taking your passport and other requested documentation.

To prove where the funds have come from, you might have to show previous tax returns, proof of a real estate sale or mortgage, and so on, depending on the source. Note that sale of stock or bonds are considered the same as cash so you will have to demonstrate where the original purchase funds came from. In short, there has to be a proportionality between the funds being transferred and the source of that money.

In reality the money laundering requirements are usually just a minor formality, however your documentation will be verified as financial institutions have to cover themselves.

The reputable houses will release your funds within 48 hours of the transfer, but I have heard of some exchange bureaus that have sat on funds for weeks before telling the client the transfer was complete - earning them a nice amount in interest no doubt. If they are doing that with all their clients imagine how much they are making!

Many private banks have now reclassified themselves as international stockbrokers, which brings them back into a gray area. Some now claim to operate a complicated system where they buy stocks for the client in the country where the funds are deposited, which are then sold immediately and the sale proceeds are given to the client in Argentina, less their dealing commission (which equates to the forex charge). This reclassification is little more than

24. Things To Organize Before The Escritura

a front so that technically they may not be breaking the law (it's very unclear), but in reality they provide the same kind of service as before; providing a quick and easy way of getting foreign currency into Argentina, and about 80% of foreigners still bring their purchase funds in this way.

Because the services these organisations provide are a grey area they tend to be shadowy and low key. You won't get anything in writing saying how they operate or confirming their commission structure. You will most likely only be given the account number of a foreign bank and a reference number with which to make your transfer. It doesn't inspire confidence.

When I bought my first property I was introduced to an apparently reputable exchange house by my friends. I was worried that they wouldn't give me anything in writing. It didn't feel right to me - it wasn't how I did business. After much agonising I decided to go ahead and use them as my friends assured me everything would be fine. I duly made the transfer, then was worried sick for the next four days (the transfer was over a weekend with a public holiday) about how stupid I had been. I had on trust transferred over US$80,000 into a black hole in Germany, with nothing in writing. My friends in the UK would think I was completely, barking mad. I thought I was completely, barking mad. Those four days were some of the most stressful of my life.

On the fourth day I got an early morning call. My funds had arrived in the bureau's German bank and the dollars were ready for me to collect from their office. My friends in Buenos Aires had been completely right and using this bureau was absolutely fine.

The Complete Guide To Real Estate Investment In Argentina

I tell you this so that you can be prepared for the stress that using a bureau may entail. In comparison to the way we do things in Europe or the US, transferring money on trust like this seems lunacy, and it's only natural that you may find it very stressful. Be prepared to deal with this. As long as you are using a reputable exchange house you have nothing to worry about.

Some exchange houses refer to themselves as private banks. They may offer pseudo-banking facilities. You won't get a cheque book, deposit book or statements, but they will hold funds on your behalf from which you can withdraw cash at any time on presentation of suitable ID. For this privilege you will pay an annual fee, typically US$50.

Some exchange houses and private banks will only accept new clients by private recommendation. As the relationship with an exchange house is based entirely on trust it is extremely important that you use one that someone you know and trust has used before, and can therefore recommend it with confidence.

It is estimated that 80% of real estate purchases by foreigners are made using funds transferred through exchange bureaus and private banks.

The supplementary appendix to this book contains details of exchange houses and private banks which are known to the reliable, honest and trustworthy.

Since 2008, as part of the government drive to encourage all foreign transactions to go through the central bank (which is claimed to be good for the economy, partly because the central bank generates money on the forex charge, and also reduces

24. Things To Organize Before The Escritura

money laundering), when a foreigner comes to sell real estate, the tax office (AFIP) now has the right to investigate whether the funds were brought into Argentina legally when the property was bought. Foreigners who cannot prove the money was brought in legally may face a fine. This is discussed further in the chapter on selling real estate.

Foreigners who use the official banking system will obviously have no problems with respect to proving the funds' provenance, so many consultants and realtors are now starting to suggest that money is brought in legally. The decision whether to use the "black" or "white" system ultimately comes down to the individual investor. The black system is currently far easier and more widely used, but there could be potential issues when it's time to sell. Over time it is expected that the white system will become easier to use, and if the proposals to make cash purchases illegal does go through then the requirements to notarize the transactions will effectively make the black system redundant.

As changing legislation is nowadays making it harder to do transactions in black, and with more potential consequences for doing so, I <u>strongly</u> recommend that all transactions are now done in white.

Carrying Cash Into The Country

Whilst I know people who have physically brought the cash to buy a property with them when they arrived in Argentina, this isn't recommended.

It's perfectly legal to bring cash into the country. Anything above US$10,000 has to be declared to customs. Customs officers have the right to search everyone and their baggage and if money is found and you haven't declared it the cash would probably be confiscated and/or you might receive a heavy fine.

On the other hand if you do declare money, it only takes one phone call from a customs officer to his associates to watch you as you go through the airport and you become a high value target for robbery.

The decision to bring in cash or not is ultimately yours, although I strongly recommend that you don't for security reasons.

Mortgage

It is difficult for local people to get mortgages. It is completely impossible for foreigners. Getting a mortgage in Argentina isn't an option.

If you need a mortgage to fund your purchase then the only way of doing so is by obtaining a mortgage on property that you already own in your home country, converting equity to cash which can then be used to purchase in Argentina.

Converting Purchase Funds Into US Dollars

If you live outside the US, the chances are that your purchase funds won't be in US dollars. Most likely they will be in pounds sterling or euros and will need converting.

Your bank will no doubt be more than happy able to convert the currency for you, but you won't get the best rate. Specialist

24. Things To Organize Before The Escritura

exchange houses exist which will give you a much better rate, especially on larger amounts. You will need to research which firms exist in your country or deal in your currency.

If you are in the UK I recommend using MoneyCorp (www.moneycorp.com) who consistently give one of the best rates on pound-dollar conversions.

The boss at one exchange house told me recently he was planning to be able to accept euros in the not-too-distant future, so if you are planning on using an exchange house it's worth asking them if they have a foreign euro account (although you need to check the euro-dollar exchange rate they will apply is ok). As the euro becomes more established and grows in popularity as a major currency around the world I can see other institutions rapidly following suit.

Cash Safety Issues - Where To Hold The Escritura Meeting

Real estate purchases in Argentina are made in cash - US dollars to be precise. It goes without saying that there are security risks involved with transporting and handling a large sum of cash needed for a purchase. You must minimize these risks.

Almost all official banks and all exchange houses will have a private room that you can book - some will let clients use it for free and some will charge a small fee, typically a few dollars.

I strongly suggest that you take advantage of this facility and arrange for the escritura meeting to be held there. That way your money is already safely in the bank or finance house and you can arrange for it to be brought into the room at the appropriate time.

The Complete Guide To Real Estate Investment In Argentina

That way there is no risk to you in transporting the cash - the risk is entirely on the seller when he takes it away.

Sometimes a seller can be awkward and insist the escritura is held somewhere else. If this happens use your common sense - don't arrange the meeting in a deserted warehouse for example. If possible try to arrange it at either your escribano or your realtor's office.

If the meeting isn't at the point where your funds have arrived into the country you are at risk, because people will know that you will be taking the cash to the meeting location at the given time. If some of these people are unscrupulous their associates may try to relieve you of it on the way. To the local people it represents a hell of a lot of money.

Tell as few people as possible you have the cash. If possible, try to take several trusted people with you when you are transporting it. Always use a *remis* or radio taxi that you have booked over the phone - that way they will have a record of the call and which driver was assigned to the job. Consider getting the driver to take an unusual or roundabout route to your destination.

Robbery of purchase funds isn't a common problem, but it can happen occasionally, usually as a result of complacency or stupidity on the part of the buyer. Use common sense and you should be fine.

Some banks provide a cash-moving service that will provide secure delivery to a given location, but this is expensive.

24. Things To Organize Before The Escritura

Title Insurance

Title insurance is principally a product developed and sold in the United States. It protects an owner's interest in real estate against loss due to title defects, liens or other matters.

Title insurance is never used by locals because the system of registration works so well, but some foreigners may feel more comfortable having it. It generally costs 0.5% of the purchase price (minimum US$850), and can be bought from several US firms such as First American (www.firstam.com). Personally, I think the use of title insurance in Argentina is unnecessary.

Warning Points for Purchasers

These are specific issues that have been drawn to my attention since the first edition of the book was published:

1. By law banks have to withhold 30% of funds transferred into the country for one year, before releasing them to the owner (Retaining capital in the country regulations). This withholding requirement is waived if it can be proved the funds are being used to purchase a property (e.g. by providing a copy of the boleto or sena). If your purchase is delayed you need to be careful that the bank doesn't then take the 30%. I've heard of a few cases where this has happened and it has proved exceedingly difficult and time-consuming to get the money credited back.

2. With new developments buyers usually have to use the developer's escribano. Often they try and charge a much higher rate, so it's worth negotiating with the developer. Developers have been known to insert a clause that makes the buyer responsible for both the buyer and seller portion of the stamp tax. Sometimes the English translation of the contract is not complete and omits this (amongst other things). It's therefore worth getting the Spanish contract properly checked out.

3). Some new build developments are slipping an inflation clause into their contracts. These typically say that the buyer agrees to pay up to a 30% inflation premium if inflation continues to go up before the project is finished. There's nothing necessarily wrong with this - inflation is a serious concern at the moment - as long as the construction company is honest and upfront about this and the buyer can make an informed decision. However, often this clause is tucked away unnoticed in the boleto or is left out of English translations. As always, the advice is to read the contract very carefully and if necessary get it independently translated.

From late 2010 there have been reports of new builds being sold with open prices, where the builder can't/won't give a final price till the building has been completed due to rising costs.

4. I've heard of buyers wanting to back out of sales because of something untoward coming to light, and losing their reserva. Here's a few tips I've come across that may help to get it back:

24. Things To Organize Before The Escritura

i). Insist that 100% of the purchase price is recorded on the title deed. If the seller refuses then you can tell them you want to back out as that is illegal. They will be obliged to give you back your money.

ii). Insist the seller must split the stamp tax (if applicable) which will cost them another 1.25%. Most owners want buyers to pay for all of it. If the reserva doesn't say anything about this tax, they are legally obligated to split it with you. Mention that and they might want to back out as well.

iii). Always make your offer conditional on the property passing an architect's inspection and the condo rules not prohibiting short-term apartment rentals.

25. Post-purchase Costs (Running Expenses)

Asset (Property) Tax

This is a tax that almost no-one will tell you about; certainly not your realtor, as they won't tell you anything that may discourage you from buying.

By law Argentineans have to pay an annual asset tax on their worldwide assets. This includes real estate, cash held, cars, boats and other high-value goods. Foreigners also have to pay this tax, but only on property they own in Argentina.

The tax is calculated based on the value of assets held at the end of each year - namely December 31st. Therefore, if you complete on a real estate transaction on say December 30th, you will be liable to pay asset tax on it for that year even though you have only owned it for a single day in that year. It is not proportioned on a pro-rata basis.

Asset tax for the previous year should be paid by May of the following year.

Many local people don't pay the asset tax and it seems many don't even know about it. It almost appears that people pay it on a voluntary basis. Incredible as it seems, no official demand or bill is sent by the tax office (AFIP) - individuals are responsible for paying the asset tax themselves. This is so fundamental I will repeat it: You will not be sent a bill but it is your responsibility to pay it.

You may be wondering that if many locals don't pay it, why should I bother? The answer is that when you want to sell your property you will have to get a certificate from the tax office stating that you are up to date on your property taxes (this is one of the

25. Post-Purchase Costs (Running expenses)

things the escribano will check for the buyer). If you haven't paid you won't be able to sell without paying the back taxes, and you will also be charged a penalty of 2% a month on the outstanding tax which will substantially increase the amount owed over time.

The government published new rates for the personal asset tax (*Impuesto a los bienes personales*) just before the presidential elections at the end of 2007, perhaps as a bit of an election bribe. The rates are not marginal rates (i.e. you don't pay a certain tax rate up to a threshold, and then a higher rate only for assets above the threshold) as under the old system. The relevant rate is charged against all assets, not just the amount over each band.

With total assets below 305,000 pesos there is no tax to pay.
Between 305,000 and 750,000 pesos the rate is 0.5%.
Between 750,000 and 2 million pesos the rate is 0.75%.
Between 2 - 5 million pesos the rate is 1%.
Over 5 million pesos the rate is 1.25%.

The above rates only apply to residents. Non-residents do not get an exemption and a flat rate of 1.25% (the top rate) is applied to all real estate owned by foreigners.

Many consultants will tell you that you need to use an accountant to work out the calculation, which you then personally have to take to the tax office on a floppy disk (and wait in line for hours) to actually pay. This may have been true in the past, but it is now possible to submit and pay online using the AFIP website.

The Complete Guide To Real Estate Investment In Argentina

To do so you will need your CDI number to create an account (remember the site is in Spanish). The system will prompt you for the relevant figures and calculate the tax for you. You probably won't know all the information (e.g. the figure to use for the land value the building is on), so I would still recommend using an accountant the first time you pay the tax as he will be able to give you the correct figures to use. Once you know these you can submit it yourself in future years.

Utility Bills (Services)

Utility bills are issued for services used by the property: namely electricity, gas, water and telephone.

In Argentina, although the utility bills come addressed to an owner, the bills are associated with the property, not the individual. If a bill isn't paid the service will simply be disconnected, regardless of who is responsible.

It is not uncommon for bills to come in the name of a previous owner who was an owner long before the person you bought from - maybe dating back twenty years or more. Since there is no credit system in Argentina sellers aren't worried about leaving their name on utility bills. If a utility isn't paid for it will simply be cut off and won't be reconnected until payment has been made.

It is possible to change the bills into your name, but the service providers don't make it easy. You usually have to go to their office in person with your passport and a copy of your title deeds. As with the tax office, you will probably have to stand in line for hours before getting served. Because it's such a time-consuming process

25. Post-Purchase Costs (Running expenses)

most people simply don't bother - after all there isn't really any need.

All utility bills have a barcode number that allows them to be paid electronically. If you have an Argentinean bank account (see later chapter) then they can be paid online via internet banking.

Alternatively, there are ubiquitous points around the city where you can pay, including the *Rapi Pago* network, most supermarket checkouts (*Pago Facil*) and of course traditional bank counters. In all these cases the barcode is scanned electronically and you hand over the cash. You are then issued with a payment receipt. The disadvantage is that frequently there are long lines at the registers and it can take ages to pay your bills. Surprisingly, this is still how most people pay - it's illogical but then people have a deep mistrust of the banking system.

Some bills have two payment dates on them. This can appear confusing at first, but actually it's to do with the fact that interest is automatically applied on overdue balances. If you pay before the first deadline you will pay the first figure; if you pay between the first and second dates you will pay the latter figure, which will include a small interest component. To give an example - $22.45 by 10th of month, or $22.90 by 30th of month.

It depends on the utility company's policy, but if you try to pay a bill after the printed deadline it may not be possible at a general bill payment point. You may have to go to a larger Rapi Pago office, whose systems are directly integrated with the utility companies' billing systems. They will therefore be able to obtain a payment figure for you which includes the applied interest up to the current date.

Sometimes you may not receive a bill (letters are delivered to the building; it is then the responsibility of the porteria to distribute individual mail items by posting them under the front door of each apartment). You may receive a notice that the service is about to be shut off. It doesn't matter to the utility company if you haven't received a bill - if the amount owed isn't paid then the service will be disconnected. It's as simple as that.

The cost of services in Argentina is very cheap compared with Europe and the US. Bills are in pesos. Obviously, the bill amount will depend on the usage, but typically most bills will equate to less than US$20 per month. In 2009 bills rose quite steeply due to the removal of some government subsidies, but they are still cheap in comparison.

Local Government Tax

All property owners pay an annual Municipal Tax, known as ABL (*alumbrado, barrido y limpieza* - lighting, sweeping and cleaning), which goes to the local government. Unlike the asset tax, you will receive a quarterly bill for the ABL, which will have an electronic payment code and can be paid in the same way as utility bills.

The ABL is worked out using factors such as building value, percentage of building occupied etc. It will already have been calculated for you. As a guide the annual ABL is now in the US$300 ballpark for most apartments (2008).

25. Post-Purchase Costs (Running expenses)

It's normal practice for the escribano to notify the ABL office of change of ownership, so the bills should come in your name automatically. If not, you will need to go to the municipal tax office armed with your passport, CDI and title documents in order to change the bill into your name.

The ABL increased by over 200% in January 2008, a change orchestrated by the new city major as part of his reform programme. However, the tax had not previously been increased for over 15 years and so had got very out of touch with reality. Even with this increase it is still a perfectly reasonable amount.

Running Costs (Expensas)

Collectively, the owners of the individual apartments in a building have the power to appoint a building manager to run the building on their behalf, as specified in the rules of the building. This manager is known as the *administracion*, or administrator. The administrator provides his services for an agreed monthly fee. The owners have the power to sack the administrator if they are unhappy with his performance.

The administrator takes responsibility for running the building. He pays the bills for the running costs including the elevators, electricity, cost of heating and hot water and the porteria's salary. He should also organize any necessary building repairs and instigate measures for preventative maintenance.

These running costs will be recouped in advance through the *expensas*, a monthly bill sent to each owner with details of the expenditure. Expensas are typically in the range of US$100 - US$200 per month, depending on the building, and are usually about the same each month. If a building has luxury facilities like a pool or a gym then the expensas will naturally be higher. Expensas are similar to a condo charge in the US.

From time to time more expensive items of maintenance will be incurred - e.g. painting the outside of the building. How this is handled depends on the building rules and the agreement with the administrator. With some buildings the owners will be charged a one-off expensa to reflect this. Other buildings may have a maintenance or reserve fund which is funded by a small premium added to the regular monthly expensas, which over time will

25. Post-Purchase Costs (Running expenses)

accumulate and should (theoretically at least) cover the cost of major items of expenditure.

The administrator will organize regular general meetings open to all apartment owners, typically every three to six months. These meetings are usually held in the lobby and are to discuss maintenance and other issues. Sometimes it may be agreed that additional expenditure will be collected through a certain number of monthly additions to the expensas, with the work commencing once the money is in place. This helps smooth the cost for the owners.

Property owners usually have three weeks to pay the expensas, after which interest will be applied in a similar fashion to utility bills.

Often cable TV is included in the expensas. Savings can be made with a whole-of-building subscription if the majority of owners have requested it, although of course individuals can choose not to receive it.

Insurance (Seguro)

By law all apartment buildings are required to have insurance cover in respect of the building as whole and covering the common areas, such as the lobby and elevators. This insurance should be automatically arranged by the administrator and reflected in the expensas.

It is not obligatory, but I would strongly advise you to take out specific insurance for your apartment, as the inside fittings and contents won't be covered under the general building policy (which only covers reconstruction of the building in the event of any incident, not the insides of individual units). Not only will you be covered in the event of fire or robbery, but you will also have civic liability cover (similar to third party liability) if someone injures themselves on your property, or if your property causes damage to another apartment - e.g. from a pipe leak, or if a fire starts in your apartment and damages another.

Insurance is inexpensive and can be bought from most banks, or direct from the insurance companies. It is also possible to buy it online from the websites of most banks. Usually, the premium is payable in monthly instalments and is paid in the same way as the utility bills.

The precise cost of insurance will depend on how much cover you need, which will be dictated by the value of your contents. Typical insurance for most apartments can be bought for between US$15 and US$20 per month.

If you are planning on renting your apartment out you should check with the insurance company that your policy is suitable. Not all policies cover the owner not being in occupation.

Ideally, you should arrange insurance cover to commence immediately after the signing of a boleto or sena, so you have cover if anything should happen to the apartment before you've taken possession of it.

Having the right insurance in place will provide good protection for your investment in case of unforeseen incidents.

26. Opening A Bank Account

Having a local bank account is useful - not only can you use it to make online payment of bills and taxes; it can also be used to receive rental income.

Opening a bank account can be difficult. Unless you are a resident it will be almost impossible until you've actually bought some real estate. Even then it's not easy.

By law the only requirement for opening a bank account is to have a CDI number, proof of address and a passport. However different banks have their own specific requirements. You would think banks would welcome you as a new customer that they will earn money from, but sadly this isn't the case. Even most multi-national banks will refuse to open accounts for non-residents.

If you already bank with a multi-national such as HSBC or Citibank in your home country that has a presence in Argentina, the local branch can usually be persuaded to open an account for you if you obtain a letter of introduction or referral from your home bank.

Remember that most bank staff won't speak English, so take someone with you that can translate when you go to open the account. You will need to take your title documents, CDI and passport. Note that although your title document will state your CDI number, due to the bureaucracy of the system this isn't sufficient and you will have to take your actual CDI certificate as well.

Your title deed provides proof of address and it is this address that the account will opened under. You can always change it at a later date if necessary once you have received the initial cashcard and other paperwork.

The Complete Guide To Real Estate Investment In Argentina

Different banks have different rules about how much you need to deposit when opening an account. Typically a hundred pesos should be enough. Some banks offer both a peso and a dollar account.

As well as transaction charges (which are minimal) banks make their money by charging a monthly maintenance fee for operating the account. Again, this varies between banks but is usually the equivalent of a couple of dollars per month.

Depending on the bank you will receive an ATM cashcard that works either on the Cirrus or Visa network. It can also be used as a debit card in stores that take Visa or Cirrus cards, although you will need to show your passport as proof of ID as this is a legal requirement in Argentina.

Note that foreigners cannot obtain credit in Argentina, so you will be unable to take advantage of your bank's loan offers, arrange an overdraft or be issued with a credit card.

27. Renting Out Property

Identifying your market

Depending on your property and its location, there are basically two options: Long-term rental to a local or corporate employee, or short-term rentals to tourists in the form of a serviced apartment. The latter option can be further subdivided into luxury rentals or standard rentals, although the line between them is often blurred.

Long-Term Rentals

Long-term rentals are traditionally what Argentineans use when they rent property. They are standard two-year rental contracts, with rent normally paid monthly in advance. Usually with long-term rentals property is let unfurnished, although *amoblado* (furnished) is also possible, but not very common.

Property rental laws in Argentina are structured to protect the tenant, not the landlord. It's possible for someone to move into a property, pay the first months rent and then pay nothing else. Landlords therefore need to do everything they can to protect themselves.

The court system is slow and it can take up to two years to have a tenant evicted, and the process is even more difficult if the tenant has children. It's almost impossible for a landlord to recoup lost rent. The possibility of this happening causes great nervousness to landlords when it comes to taking on tenants.

To mitigate this landlords almost always demand a *garantía* (guarantee). This is essentially a promise by another person that the landlord can take their property if the rent is unpaid or the tenant damages the property. It's not exactly a lien, but it gives the landlord more legal clout to recoup any losses. The person making the garantía is a *garante* (guarantor).

It can be difficult to get a garantía because the garante may be uncomfortable about risking their property should the tenant default. For this reason garantías are usually only provided to trusted family members. It is quite common for parents to provide a garantía for their children.

It is also possible for an employer to give a garantía for a trusted worker. Many multi-nationals do this when they relocate staff to Argentina.

It is up to the landlord to check out the validity of any offered garantía. If the person making it doesn't have any assets then the garantía will be useless. It's a fairly common scam for some of the less-reputable agencies to sell garantías to tenants in order for them to secure a property. These garantías are usually worthless and the tenants will have paid for nothing, and the landlord will probably get nothing if he tries to invoke it. If a garantía is offered by an agency, a diligent landlord should always get a competent lawyer to check the property register to ensure the issuer has sufficient assets to cover the garantía, and that they haven't already been pledged as garantías to other landlords - i.e. pledging the same asset to many people. (This can be implied by how many ownership detail requests have been made in a given time period.)

Because of the difficulties tenants often have obtaining a valid garantía many landlords will accept *pago adelantado*, or payment upfront (which is essentially what happens in the short-term rental

27. Renting Out Property

market). In an ideal situation the landlord would receive the full two years rent payment in advance, however two years rent is a lot of money for a local and many people may find it hard to come up with this sort of amount. For this reason, landlords sometimes accept a smaller upfront payment of say six months or a year.

If possible landlords should aim to attract corporate employees, as their companies are usually in a stronger position to pay rent upfront or provide a garantía.

With a long-term rental the tenant is usually responsible for paying the expensas and other utility bills, not the landlord.

Most long-term rentals are organized through a rental agency - these are discussed in a later section.

It is difficult to put a figure on how much rent a landlord will receive as it will depend on the area and the property, although rents have been steadily increasing in recent years. For a long-term rental the rent will be much less than for short term, and for this reason many investors prefer the short-term market.

Short-Term Rentals (Serviced Apartments)

It is the law that with short-term rentals (also known as tourist rentals) the lease can be for a maximum of six months. Property is supposed to be rented furnished and to include a refrigerator and other basic accessories as a bare minimum. What "basic accessories" are isn't defined and is up to the landlord.

Almost always the tenant will pay the rent upfront for the whole lease period on moving in. Apartments are usually priced in dollars per day, week or month and the landlord will be paid in this currency.

Sometimes landlords will sign two or more six month contracts back to back, effectively giving a longer rental period than the maximum six months. Pseudo-contracts of a year are quite common.

Depending on the property and the location, landlords may either go for the standard short-term market, or the luxury market. For the standard market the landlord will normally provide reasonable accommodation with reasonable furniture and furnishings, possibly including a television. Apartment contents should be basic but good quality and be sufficient for most tenants' needs (e.g. provision of cooking utensils).

For the luxury market the landlord will provide more. Apartments should be refurbished to the highest standard and should include luxury items such as expensive furniture (e.g. leather couches), designer kitchens, large, flat-panel TVs, DVD players and other home electronics. High speed internet access is a must. People are paying top price for quality and that's what they expect. Landlords are competing against the top-end hotels. Whilst a luxury apartment will bring in a higher rent, the initial costs in kitting it out will be significantly higher. The landlord needs to decide whether this extra expenditure is justified by considering the ROI.

In practice, the distinction between what is a luxury rental and a standard one may not be so clear cut. (See the agency section below.)

27. Renting Out Property

With short-term rentals it is the landlord's responsibility to pay the expensas and utility bills.

It is very common to restrict the phone service so that tenants can only call local numbers. Most *kioscos* (confectionary kiosks) sell a wide range of phone cards that can be used to make cheap national or international calls by dialling a local number.

The decision whether to go for short or long-term rents is ultimately the landlord's (although be aware that not all neighborhoods are suitable for short-term lets). The majority of investment landlords plump for short-term rents as the income is potentially much higher. Be aware however, that although the rent for short-term letting will be higher than with long-term letting, the occupancy rate is not guaranteed and there may be long void periods that may more than offset the higher rent. Also take into consideration that with short-term rentals the landlord is also liable for payment of the expensas and utility bills, which should be factored into any decision.

All things considered, short-term rentals are likely to be the better option for the investor, although this is by no means definite.

28. Choosing a Rental Agent *(agente de alquiler)*

It is not absolutely essential to use a rental agent (*agente de alquiler*), but they do make the process of renting your apartment much easier. Unless you live in Argentina, are familiar with the laws and have a lot of free time then I strongly recommend that you use an agent.

Having identified your market, it is important to find a rental agent that specializes in that market. For example if you have a luxury apartment you want to deal with an agent that deals primarily or exclusively with luxury apartments, not long-term lets.

Buenos Aires is awash with letting agents, almost every block seems to have one. Many of them are also realtors. In choosing one to work with the same basic principles apply as when choosing a realtor. Being able to speak the same language is crucial. You want an agent who is honest and ethical. Ask for details of other landlords they have on their books who would be happy to recommend them. Speak to these people and verify that the claims are genuine.

Some agencies are very big and will have hundreds of apartments on their books. They may do a good job, but equally the chances of getting your apartment a high occupancy rate may be less due to competition from all their other properties.

Other agencies are smaller and may target specific tenant groups, like high-end visitors, gay visitors or the European market. The chances of getting your apartment rented most of the time maybe higher with a smaller agency. The key is to look at occupancy rate and commission charged. No-one will assure you

28. Choosing A Rental Agent

an occupancy rate, but they should be able to tell you more or less their average for your kind of apartment. Bear in mind it is in their interests to inflate this figure, so don't necessarily take it at face value.

Until you have established a good relationship with an agency you should make sure you don't sign anything giving them exclusive rights to rent your apartment for a fixed time. You should always be able to change agency if you are not happy.

The commission short-term agencies usually charge is between 15% - 25% of the rental income. VAT at 21% will be added to this. Because there is good competition between the short-term agencies it is often possible to negotiate the commission rate. However, I have heard of cases where if the commission agreed is much lower than the average, the agent has given priority to other properties where they will earn a higher commission. This is something to be aware of.

Beware also that some agencies may try to charge an additional contract fee or inventory fee each time a new tenant is found. This isn't usual practice; everything is usually included in the commission percentage. Always ask an agent exactly what is and isn't included. As usual, unscrupulous people will be after your money in any way they can think of.

Some agents charge all the commission to the owner, whilst others will spit it between the owner and the tenant.

For a long-term let an agency will usually take a commission of 3% from the owner and 5% from the tenant for a 24-month contract.

Sometimes agents will ask you how much you want to charge for your apartment. I am always suspicious of this - they are supposed to be the experts so they should be the ones telling you. Ask them what their recommendation would be.

Be cautious of agencies that also own their own properties. Whilst they may tell you platitudes like they won't make any money if they don't rent your flat, the reality is that they are going to give preference to renting their own property over yours as they will make a lot more money that way.

Good agencies will have a web site from which foreigners will be able to view photos of the properties available and book online. It is worth doing some general Google searches to see if the site comes back in the results - it is good having a nice website, but only if prospective tenants can find it.

Many agents don't know how to take good photos and just point their camera around an apartment and shoot. Bad pictures don't help to rent an apartment. You may want to take your own photos that show the property in the best possible light and give them to the agent. Photos taken at different times of the day may show different rooms at their best - e.g. sunlight streaming through a window.

As well as finding tenants an agency will take care of the day-to-day management of the property. Depending on the level of service required this can include organising repairs and general maintenance of the apartment and arranging cleaning and fresh laundry between tenancies. It can also include payment of all utility bills etc. and the expansas on behalf of the landlord. A monthly fee

28. Choosing A Rental Agent

is usually charged for doing this, which can be quite high, often upwards of US$70 - plus VAT. This kind of service is invaluable for landlords resident overseas.

The agency will also deal with the tenant check-ins and check-outs. They will hold the tenant's security deposit and check the inventory on departure.

Some of the top-end agencies provide a more tailor-made service to tenants and will pick them up and drop them off at the airport, for example. Some agencies also provide a maid service (i.e. regular cleaning) for tenants - at the landlord's expense. Such services are of course factored into the rent charged.

Agencies cannot guarantee occupancy, and the better ones will tell you themselves that you will increase your chances of letting if you use more than one agency. Most agencies are happy for you to do this - be very suspicious of any that require you to use them as the sole agent.

Normally where more than one agency is used, one acts as a kind of master agency and will be responsible for maintenance (and possibly paying the landlord's bills). The other agency(ies) will only find and check-in/out tenants. Obviously, you need to ensure that there is a good line of communication between the different parties to prevent double booking.

The supplementary appendix to this book contains details of a number of agencies specialising in different markets who are known to be reliable and honest.

29. Taxation Issues

The treatment of tax is complex, but there are accepted rules which make dealing with it straightforward for foreigners.

Rental income is subject to national income tax, currently at a rate of 35%. The tax must be withheld at the time of rent payment if it is destined for a foreign recipient. The property manager (rental agency) is responsible for withholding the tax.

The foreign recipient can decide the taxable basis on which the withholding should be made. There are two options:

General Rule: This uses the legally prescribed assumption that taxable income will account for 60% of the rent paid. This results in an effective withholding rate of 21% of the total, derived from the application of the 35% tax rate upon a 60% notional income.

Specific Rule: The tax paid is calculated by deducting the actual expenses incurred in Argentina which are necessary for obtaining and maintaining the income or preserving its source, and deducting other allowances permitted under the law from the gross rent.

In short, you can pay a withholding tax of 21% of the rent, or work out the actual profit and pay tax on that at 35%.

If you take the latter route, you will need to hire an accountant to work out the correct figure taking into account deductions and other expenses allowable by law. You may end up paying more than an effective rate of 21%. The legal assumption that taxable income will account for 60% of the rent is about right, so the tax

29. Taxation Issues

figure is likely to be in this ballpark. Don't forget that an accountant will also charge you a nice fee for working this out.

For these reasons, it is much easier just to let the agent withhold 21% of the rent and pay the tax on your behalf. I strongly recommend you take this option.

Most agents will only deal with landlords on a 21% withholding tax basis. The other option involves more work for them and they could be at risk if the tax isn't paid. By simply withholding 21% they know they are covered.

The income tax described above refers to taxation at the national level. At provincial level rental income is subject to gross revenue tax. Rental income paid to private individuals is exempt, provided the maximum number of rented properties does not exceed the maximum established by each jurisdiction (two in the Capital Federal). The tax rates levied on rental income where the landlord exceeds the number of exempt properties typically range between 3% and 5% depending on the jurisdiction.

If a property is owned by a corporation then tax will be calculated based on the company's annual profits, in accordance with the rules and rates in place at the time. Discussion of corporation tax is outside the scope of this book.

All companies are subject to *Ganancia Mínima Presunta* (Presumed Minimum Gain) tax. This is an annual asset tax equivalent to 1% of the value of a company's assets (e.g. property). This tax is complementary to corporation tax and companies are required to pay whichever is the greater of the two.

Depending on the province, rental contracts may be subject to stamp duty. Rates are typically between 0.5% and 2.5%. In the Capital Federal stamp tax on rental contracts has been abolished.

All agency fees and commissions are classified as professional services and are subject to VAT at 21%.

If you are not living in Argentina you may need to appoint someone to represent you when submitting your annual tax return. Usually this would be your accountant. Typically you can expect to pay US$100 upwards for this kind of service.

Depending where you reside, you may be legally obliged to declare earnings in Argentina in your home country and potentially to pay tax on them. Double taxation is a situation in which taxes are paid twice on the same income due to an overlap between different countries' tax laws and jurisdictions. As this is inequitable, many nations enter into double taxation treaties that ensure such tax is only paid once. Argentina has double taxation treaties with most countries so double taxation is unlikely to be an issue.

All countries in the world revise their tax laws and rates from time to time. Argentina is no exception.

30. Refurbishing Real Estate

If you are renting towards the upper end of the market your property will need to be in an excellent condition. If it is not, you will have to undertake some refurbishment (*remodelar*). You may also want to refurbish a property if you are going to be living in it yourself. What refurbishment is necessary will depend on the state of the property.

Redecorating

At the very least you may want to give your new property a coat of paint to smarten it up. This is cheap and easy enough to do yourself if you want. Buenos Aires is littered with stores that sell paint and it is inexpensive. You can get an odd-job man to do it for under a couple of hundred dollars.

Color is a matter of personal taste of course, but I recommend painting in light, neutral colors. This will look smart and will appeal to the majority of tenants, who may very well be put off by that garish purple or whatever color that you like so much yourself. Even if you don't think your property needs redecorating, I still recommend doing it as it will make the place look much smarter. The smarter the property the more tenants tend to take care of it.

Natural wear and tear takes a toll on the condition of the paintwork. There's no hard and fast rule, but on average I would plan on redecorating an apartment approximately every 5 years.

Floor Restoration

Tenants like smart wooden floors. If an existing parquet floor is looking a bit tired and tatty then you can have it restored. This involves having the existing varnish and dirt sanded off down to the clean wood below. The freshly exposed wood is then stained to the required color and lacquered with a plastic protection layer (plastificado). Costs for doing this are around US$12 per square metre of flooring. There are a number of firms in Buenos Aires that do this, so get different quotes. Try to go with a firm that someone has recommended as doing a good job.

Note that floor restoration is an extremely messy process. The industrial sanding machines produce a vast amount of extremely fine dust which settles everywhere and takes an age to get rid of properly. For this reason have the floor restored before any decorating is done. Restoration normally takes two days - the first day is for the preparation (sanding), the second for the staining and lacquering. Once the wood has been sanded you must not walk on it before it is lacquered as this may damage it. The lacquer emits fumes and takes a day to dry thoroughly, so you can't live in an apartment whilst the restoration is going on.

Most restoration firms provide a ten year guarantee. The floor should last at least twenty years before the process needs doing again, indeed some floors in good condition are considerably older and may never have been restored.

30. Refurbishing Real Estate

Kitchens, Bathrooms and Building Work

If the kitchen and bathroom are old and beat up they will need replacing. The insides of some apartments in Buenos Aires look distinctly 1970s, with lurid color schemes such as avocado green, mustard yellow or chocolate brown. Tenants like a nice modern feel with simple lines and clean white porcelain.

Be aware that ripping a bathroom or kitchen out and replacing it is not a simple job, and will almost certainly take much longer than it would in your home country. For a start most bathrooms and kitchens are tiled floor to ceiling and the old tiles will have to be hacked off. Note that construction methods are different in Argentina and tiles are not generally glued onto the wall, but concreted on. When the old tiles come off they will pull off the concrete adhesive which in turn will bring off lumps of the render underneath.

Once the room has been stripped it will be necessary to re-render the walls before they can be retiled. Depending on the speed of the workmanship, this may take several days. Some workman still mix concrete and render by hand in a small bucket, which is a slow process.

Bathroom and kitchen floors are usually ceramically tiled as well, so the above process will have to be repeated to provide a new floor. Occasionally it may be feasible to lay new floor tiles directly onto the old ones without ripping them out, if they are flat and solid.

It is important to note that the artificial lighting under which tiles are displayed in many stores can give a false indication of color. I know of one lady who chose tiles for her kitchen. She was out when they were delivered, but the tiler was waiting for them and started putting them up. When she returned she discovered they were a rather different color to what she had bought. Furious, she phoned me and we took a box back to the store. We marched up to the display with the assistant and held up a tile they had supplied next to it. To our horror, they were exactly the same color. I have found this problem to be quite common, so always try to see what the tiles look like under natural daylight before buying. Often stores will tell you that this is not possible, but if you are persistent they can usually be persuaded to go into the back room and fetch a single tile for you to take outside.

Many older apartment buildings were literally built around the bath. Some apartments have cast iron baths which were set in position and the building was constructed around them. They are too big and heavy to take out in one piece, so after the supporting masonry has been hacked away they will need cutting into smaller pieces. Even a third of a bath can be difficult for two men to lift, the iron is typically a centimetre (just under half an inch) thick or more.

Modern European and most US baths are supported on a metal frame that has adjustable legs that are screwed in or out to level the tub to the correct position. Not so in Argentina. A bathtub is just a bathtub, and they are set in place by packing concrete under them. Depending on the workers, the mixing of concrete and setting of the tub in position may take several days. Once the concrete is dry the side of the bath can be tiled. Note that there is no access requirement as the taps do not come from under the

30. Refurbishing Real Estate

bath itself but out of the wall above, like the baths in many hotel chains.

Although there are firms that specialize in kitchen or bathroom refurbishment, using them tends to be a more expensive option. I've found that tradesmen in Buenos Aires have networks of other tradesmen that are friends or associates. This means that you can contract with (say) your favorite electrician or plumber to put in your complete new bathroom, and they will use people from their associate network to complete the other parts of the operation that are outside their areas of skill (e.g. tiling, building, electrical work or plumbing). In practice many tradesmen are multi-skilled, so an electrician may well do plumbing work as well, for example.

Your chosen tradesman will be your main point of contact. He will go away and consult with his colleagues before giving you a price. You may be given an approximate estimate based on the number of days the job should take, or you may be given a fixed price. I suggest you always press for a fixed price. Different tradesmen work at vastly different speeds and estimates of how long something will take can prove very wrong. I know of one person who had a new bathroom put in, which was supposed to take two days to retile. In fact it took two weeks because the tiler was incredibly slow, although he did a good job. Fortunately the apartment owner was paying for the job and not by the day.

The other thing to be clear about is whether the job includes materials or not. Usually the apartment owner buys the obvious components like the tiles, kitchen and bathroom units etc. But there will be other less obvious materials needed, such as sand, cement, pipes and wiring etc. Normally these items will be supplied by the tradesmen, as they will have an accurate idea of what's required. Sometimes the price quoted will include these, other times they will be additional.

If materials are additional, you must stress the importance of providing receipts for what has been bought and being able to accurately explain where the materials have been used, before you will reimburse for them. It is tempting for some tradesmen to see wealthy (in their mind) foreigners as a cash cow.

If the work involves anything to do with a gas supply (e.g. moving pipes, connecting new appliances) make sure the person doing this particular part of the job has a competence certificate permitting them to work with gas (similar to CORGI registration in the UK).

There are many stores that sell fitted kitchens. When buying a new kitchen it is usual practice that the kitchen will be "made ready" before the kitchen firm fits the units. What "made ready" means is that all gas, electrical and water points will be correctly positioned as per the kitchen company's plan and the kitchen will have been completely retiled. It is then a simple (usually half day) job for the kitchen company to come along and drop their custom made units into place.

Lead times for new kitchens are typically 4-6 weeks. Prices for kitchens are broadly similar between different companies, but the quality varies considerably. Have a good look at what you are being sold - are those doors solid wood or cheap laminate? Although the kitchen company will often offer to do the work to make the kitchen

30. Refurbishing Real Estate

ready for their units (perhaps via an associate company) it is almost always cheaper to get it done using a favored local tradesman and his network.

Unlike kitchens, with bathrooms most components are standard and are usually available from stock. There are many small stores that sell baths, bidets, basins and toilets as do the big DIY chains like Easy.

Having a new kitchen or bathroom installed is considerably cheaper than doing so in Europe or the US. Whilst it's impossible to give an exact price because each job will be different, typical figures are likely to be in the US$4,000 - US$9,000 ballpark, although you can spend far more than this if you want to.

The key with all refurbishment work is being able to communicate with the person responsible for the refurbishment in a language that you are comfortable with, to avoid confusion and complications. Most tradesmen do not understand English.

A good property consultant should be able to help you with refurbishment, if you are using one. Some consultants will just recommend you to trusted workmen and others will go the whole hog and act as a complete project manager for you if you require this. Typically they charge around US$4,000 for providing this kind of service. Be aware that the people they recommend or contract to do the work may not necessarily be the cheapest, and they may well be getting some kind of kickback. Always make sure you clarify the exact cost before any work commences.

Some consultants charge a percentage of the value of the work undertaken - 10% is common. If you are charged a percentage-based fee it is in the consultant's interest for the works to be as expensive as possible, so be aware that they may not necessarily have your best interests at heart.

The supplementary appendix to this book contains details of reliable and trusted tradesmen in Buenos Aires. It also contains a section on specific recommended places to go to buy tiles, kitchens and bathrooms.

31. Furnishing Property

Long-term lets are usually on an unfurnished basis, but if you are going to rent a place out on a short-term basis you will need to furnish it, as of course you will if you plan to live in it yourself.

From a rental point of view you don't need to go overboard. Simple, good-quality basics will be sufficient. If you are aiming towards the upper end of the market (as the majority of foreign landlords will be) then you need the following as a minimum:

Bedrooms

You will need to provide a bed, bedside tables with lamps, a wardrobe if there isn't one built in, and a full-length mirror (on the bedroom door always looks good). Optionally, you might like to consider a chest of drawers or dressing table if there is room. It is usual practice to supply two sets of sheets per bed and two pillows per potential bed occupant.

Lounge/Sitting Room

You will need to provide a sofa and comfortable seating for at least the apartment's maximum occupancy figure. Ideally there should be coffee or small side tables where people can easily reach drinks from where they are sitting. Depending on the market you are aiming at you may want to supply a TV, DVD player and a stereo system.

Dining Area

You will need to provide a table with at least as many chairs as the apartment's maximum occupancy figure. It's also a good idea to provide place (setting) mats.

Bathroom

The bathroom should be equipped with a shower curtain or screen, mirror, towel holders, toilet paper holder, toilet brush and a small trash can. There should be hooks for robes on the back of the door. It is usual practice to supply two bath towels and two hand towels per person for the maximum occupancy figure.

Kitchen

The kitchen should have a hob and an oven. A fridge, preferably a fridge/freezer, and a microwave oven are standard, as is a trash bin.

You need to provide as a minimum one set of crockery and cutlery per person for the maximum occupancy figure. You must also provide a pan set (saucepans, frying pan etc.) and cooking utensils such as spoons, spatulas and a colander.

A coffee maker is essential, as is a toaster and a kettle. (Kettles that sit on the stove are the norm and it can be hard to find an electric one, although not impossible.)

31. Furnishing Property

Exterior

If the apartment has a balcony or outside area then you should provide an outdoor table and enough seats to satisfy the minimum occupancy figure (provided there is sufficient space).

Adding plants is a nice touch, but consider the practicalities of getting them watered regularly.

General

Most apartments have a phone. Have the line restricted so tenants can only make local calls - they can make other calls by using a cheap calling card. These days many apartments provide high-speed internet access, either from a broadband connection or wirelessly via a wifi box.

Most apartments have air conditioning or at the very least ceiling fans. This is important for rentals in the summer months. Most windows will have shutters, if not you will need to provide curtains or blinds - you may wish to provide these anyway if you are aiming more upmarket.

You should provide basic cleaning equipment - brush, pan, mop and bucket etc. If you have carpets then include a vacuum cleaner. Although the tenants may not use this equipment, the maid that comes to clean between tenancies will need it.

Tenants will look after a place much better if they are made to feel welcome. This means thinking about the little finishing touches. It includes putting pictures on the walls, maybe a few colorful cushions on the sofa and perhaps an attractive throw or cover on the beds. A few inexpensive ornaments don't hurt or even a vase of flowers. You don't have to go over the top - just go into each room and think about what little touches you would make if you were your home to give it that lived-in feeling (but don't clutter).

Your apartment will be in competition with others. Tenants judge prospective apartments by the photos they see - so if yours looks more homely and has better finishing touches then a tenant is more likely to want it and you will boost your occupancy rate.

I recommend leaving a folder in the apartment giving information in English about the apartment - e.g. where to empty the trash, basic instructions on how to operate the appliances and air conditioning, where to buy and how to use phone cards, and how to configure a laptop to work with the internet connection. It is a good idea to include local information - e.g. where is the nearest supermarket, chemist (pharmacy), ATM, *lavanderia* (laundry) etc.

It's also a nice touch to leave basic tourist information, including leaflets, brochures and local maps which can be obtained from the city's tourist offices.

Buying Furniture

There are plenty of stores that sell furniture in Buenos Aires. Often stores selling similar types of furniture are located almost next door to each other in the same neighborhood, creating a kind of mini-quarter for that kind of item (e.g. tables and chairs).

Unlike the US and most of Europe, you can't just walk into a furniture store in Argentina and buy immediately. The majority are little more than showrooms and carry no stock. You will have to order what you want and pay 50% as a deposit. The goods will

31. Furnishing Property

then be specifically manufactured - typically it takes around four to six weeks before you will take delivery.

There are some stores that carry furniture in stock; commonly stuff that has been imported from China. It is usually very cheap and not at all well made. You can tell this by look and feel of it. It won't last long before it falls apart. Such furniture is also designed for much lighter bodies than most Americans or Europeans have and simply won't take the weight. Buying furniture from these places is a false economy.

All stores will arrange *flete* (delivery) for a small fee, typically US$10 - US$15.

Quality furniture is not as cheap as most people expect, but will still be cheaper than comparable stuff in your home country. As a rough ballpark figure you can expect to pay US$900 for a bed, US$600 for a sofa and US$350 for a table and four chairs. Electrical goods such as TVs will cost the same or more due to higher taxes.

Reasonable quality kitchen equipment can be bought from the larger supermarket chains, such as Carrefour, Jumbo or Norte.

Tigre is a satellite town located about 20km from Buenos Aires. It is well known for having many small workshops that make furniture. It is a good place to source inexpensive wooden furniture including outdoor tables and chairs.

To fully furnish an average one bedroom apartment expect to pay in the region of US$4,500 - US$8,000, although you can pay a lot more than this if you buy the most expensive items.

The Complete Guide To Real Estate Investment In Argentina

Whilst you can buy furniture yourself it can be a time consuming business to find what you want. There is also going to be a lot of time spent sitting around waiting for it to be delivered. Property consultants will often help you source furniture, as will some rental agencies, although expect to pay upwards of US$1,000 for the pleasure.

The supplementary appendix to this book contains a list of stores that are known to provide good quality furniture at a reasonable price.

32. Sample ROI calculation

Now that all the factors related to purchasing and equipping a property ready for rental have been explained, it is an appropriate point to consider a sample return on investment calculation.

We will assume you are interested in buying a 60 square metre apartment in downtown Buenos Aires for US$90,000, which includes 2.5% stamp tax. The apartment needs decorating at a cost of US$500, but otherwise needs no other refurbishment. It will also need furnishing at an approximate cost of US$5,000.

Apartment Price (inc. stamp tax)	US$ 90,000
Realtor fee @ 3% plus 21% VAT	US$ 2,699
Escribano fee @ 2.5% (all inclusive) plus 21% VAT	US$ 2,179
Money transfer fee of 2% using private bank	US$ 1,800
Refurbishment (redecorating)	US$ 500
Cost of furnishing ready for rental	US$ 5,000
Total cost of acquiring property ready to rent:	US$102,178

Next, we need to look at the likely rental income. After talking to several hypothetical agents we decide that US$1,500 per month is realistic for a short-term rent. We will assume a 70% occupancy rate and that the annual running costs will equate to US$1,500.

The Gross Annual Rent is therefore US$1,500 x 12 x 70% = US$12,600

The Complete Guide To Real Estate Investment In Argentina

From this we must deduct costs that will be incurred:

20% agency commission, plus 21% VAT	US$3,049
Running costs (expensas and utility bills etc)	US$1,500
Annual asset tax @ 0.75% of purchase price	US$675

This leaves a net profit of US$7,376 before income tax.

The ROI before tax is then (US$7,376 / US$102, 178) * 100 = 7.22%

Assuming income tax is withheld at 21% by the agency, then the net profit after tax is US$7,376- US$2,646 = US$4,730 which gives an ROI after tax of 4.63%

The investor would need to consider whether an ROI of 4.63% was sufficient in comparison to other potential uses the capital.

The above example makes many assumptions. Changing some of the values will lead to a different ROI. For example, changing the occupancy rate to 60% drops the post-tax ROI to 3.7%, whilst an occupancy rate of 40% gives only 1.8%. Using an agency fee of 25% gives 3.9%. If the monthly rent were only US$1,000 then the ROI is reduced to 2.9%.

To fully understand the implications of a potential investment, you are advised to build a simple spreadsheet model similar to the above. You can then play around with the different variables to see

32. Sample ROI Calculation

what effect they have and see what happens to the ROI if you make different assumptions.

Note that there are many ways to interpret numbers and the above example is meant as an illustrative guide only. It is somewhat simplified, but is adequate for the intended purpose. The more mathematically advanced investor may additionally take into account factors such as depreciation on fixtures and furniture, amortized cost of future refurbishments etc. These topics are beyond the scope of this book.

33. Investing In Real Estate Outside Of Buenos Aires

The vast majority of foreign investors purchase real estate in the Capital Federal. However, Argentina is a beautiful country and there are many other popular places beyond the capital where foreigners tend to buy.

These include houses and apartments in the large cities of Mendoza and Cordoba, holiday accommodation on the Atlantic coast at Mar del Plata, and farms or ranches down south in Patagonia. Foreigners also buy wineries and vineyards in Mendoza province, ski chalets in the Andes and lakeside homes in the foothills.

Some of these real estate opportunities will be businesses, subject to specific employment, tax, accounting and other rules. Discussion of real estate that forms part of a business (except rental income from residential units) is beyond the scope of this book and you should always seek professional advice from someone involved with the particular industry in question before buying. Realtor fees for purchasing commercial property are typically 4-5%, however for farms and vineyards 3% is the norm.

Although this book is Buenos Aires-centric, the information in it is just as valid for people buying in other parts of Argentina. The legal process is the same, and you need to take the same care when it comes to selecting realtors, escribanos and consultants etc. The factors to consider in relation to apartments are just as valid in other cities as they are in Buenos Aires.

33. Investing In Real Estate Outside Of Buenos Aires

However, different provinces and *departamentos* may have their own local laws and there may be minor differences compared with buying in the capital, particularly with regard to local taxes. For example, different municipalities levy different stamp duty rates on real estate purchases and provincial income tax may be charged on rental income over and above the federal rate.

In a few municipalities like Bariloche, foreigners are required to obtain a permit from the local authority before being allowed to purchase property. This can be a lengthy process and can take a year or more. Permits are normally given if can be established that a transaction with a foreigner will benefit the local community. Usually, being able to demonstrate that you are going to invest money in building or extending a house which will use local labor and supplies will be sufficient. If a permit is necessary I would advise you to use the services of a local person to help guide you through the bureaucracy of the process and to help with your application.

If permission cannot be obtained it may still be possible to purchase the real estate through a company or via setting up a trust. Again, you would need to seek local professional advice.

It is beyond the scope of this book to be able to give detailed tax and other local information about all of Argentina's 23 provinces and the dozens of municipalities that each contains. Should you wish to invest in these areas then you will need to make your own enquires as to the specific rules and tax rates applicable in your chosen location. Local realtors should be able to supply this information.

34. Multiple Property Ownership

There is no limit to the number of properties an individual can own in Argentina. There are, however, some tax implications.

If a buyer already has property in a jurisdiction then stamp tax is due on each additional property purchased in that jurisdiction. This is 2.5% of the sale price in Buenos Aires, and typically between 1 – 4% in other areas.

At the provincial level, rental income is subject to gross revenue tax. Rental income paid to private individuals is exempt, provided the maximum number of rented properties does not exceed the maximum established by each jurisdiction. In the Capital Federal this is currently two units.

35. Selling Real Estate

Sooner or later an investor may want to sell their property, perhaps to free up capital or realize a gain from an increase in value.

Since 2008 revised COTI regulations (*Código de oferta de transferencia de inmuebles*) mean a permit is now required from AFIP before a property can be legally put on the market. This applies to both nationals and foreign owners. The owner states how much the sale price should be, and the permit allows the sale of that property within a given margin of the stated value. The permit is valid for 24 months. The new regulations require all realtors and notaries to report to AFIP all properties that they sell and for how much. If the reported price is outside of what is considered an acceptable margin in relation to the permit price then AFIP will investigate the transaction. This process is designed to stop under-reporting of the sale price and hence the asset tax payable in the future.

In many ways the process of selling is the reverse of the buying process. You won't need a consultant, but you will need a realtor (unless you are planning on selling direct yourself through the newspapers, which I don't recommend).

You need an honest and ethical realtor and the same general cautions apply to selecting one as when you are a buyer. See the *How to Choose a Realtor* chapter for details.

A realtor may tell you that your property is worth considerably more than it is. By leading you to believe that they can obtain a higher price than other realtors they hope you will give your business to them. This is a common problem with realtors and is

The Complete Guide To Real Estate Investment In Argentina

not just confined to Argentina, it happens in most places. You will have to talk to several realtors and make your own value judgement.

The realtor will be responsible for marketing the apartment for you. The selling fee will typically be 3% and you need to ascertain exactly what this fee will include - some realtors may try to make you pay for the costs of placing newspaper advertisements or printing promotional materials.

Many realtors don't seem to know how to take good photos and will just point their camera around an apartment and click. Bad pictures won't help sell your apartment. You may want to take your own photos that show the property in the best possible light and give them to your realtor. Photos taken at different times of the day may show different rooms at their best - e.g. sunlight pouring in.

The realtor will only be paid their fee once the boleto is signed, so they have an incentive to work hard to try to sell the property. They are responsible for reporting offers to you, but again be mindful of the pitfalls identified in the buying chapters and be aware that not all offers may be passed on.

Once an offer is agreed you will either sign a boleto, or go straight to escritura with the option of signing a sena. You will take possession of any funds paid by the buyer at this point. It is important that you fulfil your obligation to transfer the property to the buyer on the stipulated date otherwise you will have to refund the money, and double it.

The seller doesn't choose the escribano, the buyer does. The seller will need to provide the escribano with a certificate from the

35. Selling Real Estate

tax office (AFIP) showing that the asset tax payments are up to date. Obtaining this may take a month or more. (Note that this is different from the AFIP permit to sell). You can't actually apply for the certificate before you have an offer to purchase the property, unless you have a residency visa. If the taxes are not up to date you will have to pay the back taxes plus a fine that could be up to 25% of the amount owed.

Be aware that the tax office has the right to check the utility records to see who has been living in a property. If they decide the property has been rented and the owner hasn't paid the rental taxes then the tax office will assess what it believes is owed.

As well as the tax certificate, the seller will have to prove to the escribano that all the utility and municipal taxes are up to date, as per the escritura section.

If selling as a private individual there is no capital gains tax to pay. (I've heard it said that Argentina has zero capital gains tax because the affluent who control the power are big property owners.) However, you may technically be liable to pay tax in your home country, depending on its tax rules.

Instead of capital gains tax, sellers have to pay a tax of 1.5% of the sale price, called Transfer Tax. Reducing this tax is one of the reasons owners like to under-record the true value of a sale. The tax is waived if it is the seller's main residence in Argentina and the seller is using the proceeds immediately to purchase another property. However, since March 2008, this has had to be proved and unless the seller has obtained a waiver permit from AFIP proving that they are buying another property, the escribano is legally obliged to withhold the tax from the sale proceeds.

In Buenos Aires there is no local stamp tax for buying a first residential property under US$120,000 (provided the purchaser is a national), although in other provinces the rate may vary between 1% - 4%, depending on the jurisdiction. Keep in mind the stamp tax is technically the buyer's responsibility, but it is commonly split 50:50 and this often forms part of the offer agreement.

As a foreign seller, you may not want to be paid in cash (unless you are under-reporting the sale price), and have to deal with the security headaches that cash entails. It may be easier for the buyer to wire funds direct to your overseas bank account. This involves the buyer having to obtain notarized documentation that the funds have been transferred. Note that there will be some foreign exchange transaction charges which will reduce the value of the funds sent, so it should be made a condition of the offer acceptance which party will be responsible for bearing the cost of this. Sellers try to shunt it onto the buyer, and vice-versa, so it's important to agree.

The best option currently is probably that the seller is paid in cash, which is then wired abroad through a private bank. To send money out of Argentina in this way should cost no more than 0.5%.

Note that since the start of 2008, when a foreigner comes to sell real estate purchased after 2006, the tax office (AFIP) now has the right to investigate whether the funds were brought into Argentina legally when the property was bought, specifically whether money laundering regulations were followed. Foreigners who cannot prove

35. Selling Real Estate

the money was brought in legally could face a fine or further investigation.

The tax office reserves the right to investigate, but that does not mean that they necessarily will. Depending on an individual's circumstances, it may be very hard for them to prove money has come in illegally. For example, it's possible to bring US$10,000 into Argentina on each visit without declaring it. If you have made several trips before buying you could have brought this amount with you each time, and if you had friends or family who also visited Argentina they could have brought money with them as well. To prove otherwise could be very difficult. There are many other "inventive" ways that could be used to explain how money has come in "legally".

The reclassification of many private banks as international stock brokers means that money transferred through them is once again a gray area of the law. It is not yet clear whether using one would be classed as bringing the funds in legally or not.

Since 2008 all financial institutions (including stock brokers, exchange houses etc.) have had to ensure all money transfers through them follow revised money laundering regulations – i.e. the source of funds can be proved. My understanding is that AFIP are mainly concerned with this money laundering aspect of the legality and demonstrating the source of funds was legal.

36. Residency And Citizenship

In you plan to live in your property, you may want to consider becoming officially resident in Argentina. Although you can stay indefinitely on a tourist visa (provided you leave and re-enter the country every 90 days), having official residency can have its advantages.

For a start you will get a DNI *(Documento Nacional de Identidad)*, Argentina's national identity document. It is a small booklet that includes information about your identity, including a number that uniquely identifies you. DNI numbers are an essential part of life in Argentina and are needed for many transactions, particularly where contracts are involved, and for interactions with government and the banking system. Although a passport can sometimes be used instead, showing a DNI is much easier. Foreigners with a DNI are entitled to the same rights (except voting) and legal protections as Argentinean citizens, whereas those without a DNI are not.

The way to obtain a DNI is through acquiring temporary or permanent residency. Residency is obtained through the issuing of a visa which is stamped in your passport.

Although many different types of residency visa exist (e.g. student) the most appropriate ones for the real estate investor are outlined below:

Financier

This is a very broad and flexible visa. The applicant must prove that they have a guaranteed income of $2600 pesos per month (approx

36. Residency And Citizenship

US$850) and that this income can be transferred to an Argentinean bank. The income can come from an annuity, as a beneficiary under a trust, or receipts from your own business. You must prove that the income is not tied to a job located abroad and that the income stream will continue once you relocate to Argentina.

Immigrant with Capital

This visa requires the investment of at least $150,000 pesos (approx US$50,000) in a productive activity. This could include buying agricultural land that produces an annual harvest, or a ranch that produces milk or beef. Investment of the funds in other types of business venture is also possible. Note however that the acquisition of residential property for your own use does not qualify.

Pensioner

If you are receiving a pension from your home country you should qualify if you can prove that your monthly income is at least $2100 pesos (approx US$700) and that the money can be paid into an Argentinean bank account.

Contracted Personnel

This visa is normally issued if you have obtained a job offer from a company in Argentina. However, I have heard of it being used where a foreign individual has incorporated an Argentinean company and created a position that requires the appointment of themselves, and have issued an appointment letter which is used to apply for the visa. This is stretching the rules a bit, but apparently does happen.

All visas need to be applied for from your home country and typically take at least three-plus months to process. As well as paying an application fee, you will need to supply a police certificate stating that you are free of criminal conviction, birth and marriage certificates and certification from a doctor stating that you are free of contagious diseases. All documentation must be apostilled (officially certified). You will also be required to attend an interview at the consular section of the Argentinean embassy in your home country.

Initial residency visas are issued on a temporary basis. All visas must be renewed twice before you can be issued with a permanent visa. (In certain situations the Immigrant with Capital visa can be issued permanently.)

As a permanent resident in Argentina you would be taxed on your worldwide income. However if you do not generate actual income in Argentina then you do not have to pay taxes over income generated abroad - i.e. if you simply want to live in Argentina and you generate income from business assets, investments or pensions that are based in your home country you will not be required to pay income taxes in Argentina.

After you have had residency status for five years you can apply for citizenship. If this is granted you will become a naturalized citizen and can apply for an Argentinean passport. Note that whilst

36. Residency And Citizenship

many countries allow dual nationality, the US does not, so US citizens would officially be required to give up their US nationality.

Further details can be obtained from the consular section of the Argentinean embassy in your home country.

37. Death And Inheritance *(sucesion)*

In most countries you write a will which describes in legal form how you want your estate (assets) to be divided on your death. You are usually free to distribute your property as you see fit.

In Argentina the situation is different. The concept of family rates highly on the agenda and you can only specify what happens to your assets through a will in certain circumstances. The bulk of your estate will automatically go to your family regardless of whether you specify otherwise in your will. This includes real estate.

If you die leaving a spouse and children your personal assets (i.e. those typically acquired before you got married) are split between your spouse and children in equal parts. For assets that are jointly owned by the deceased and spouse, the percentage owned by the deceased is split 50% with the spouse and 50% with the children (e.g. if the parents owned everything on a 50-50 basis, then the surviving spouse would end up with 75% of the whole and the children 25%). The assets given to children are split equally amongst siblings.

If you don't have any children then everything goes to the spouse. If you are single then your assets pass to your parents.

If you are not married, have no children or parents then you are free to leave your assets to whomever you like in a will. If you have no immediate family and you die intestate (without leaving a will) then other relatives can lay claim to your assets. The pecking-order is defined in law and goes brothers and sisters, aunts and uncles,

37. Death And Inheritance

and finally inlaws. The laws governing this are quite complex and prescriptive, but this is essentially what they boil down to.

Should you have no family capable of inheriting then your property goes to the State to be sold for the benefit of educational projects.

If you own property as a private individual in Argentina, it will be subject to these rules on your death. If you are resident in Argentina and living in the property then there is no way round them. Usually, however, people want to leave their assets to their family so this isn't often a problem.

However, if you are not a resident and are normally resident in your home country (e.g. you just own the property as an investment) then it may be possible to get a court order in Argentina giving your executors leave to deal with your Argentinean assets under any will they are administrating in your home country.

Note that Argentina has no death duties or inheritance tax and the whole value of the estate is passed to heirs.

The Complete Guide To Real Estate Investment In Argentina

38. Glossary

ABL (*alumbrado, barrido y limpieza*)	Municipal tax (similar to council tax in the UK)
abogado (a)	Spanish for lawyer
Administacion	Administrator collectively appointed by owners of residential units to run the building on their behalf
Administración Federal de Ingresos Públicos (AFIP)	Argentina's tax office
Administrator	See *administracion*
agente de alquiler	Rental agency
asset tax	Annual wealth tax on property (foreigners now pay a flat rate of 1.25%)
Barrio	Spanish for neighborhood
Barrio Norte	Informal name given to parts of Retiro, Recoleta, Balvanera and Palermo centring around Av Santa Fe
Belgrano	Leafy upper-middle class barrio to the north of Buenos Aires
boleto de compraventa	A contract between the buyer and seller. The seller obligates himself to transfer the property to the buyer on a given date, and the buyer agrees to pay for the property on that date. It regulates the conditions of the sale
capital appreciation	A rise in the market price of an asset
Capital Federal	The federal heart of Buenos Aires
capital gains tax (CGT)	A tax charged on capital gains, the profit realized on the sale of an asset that was purchased at a lower price

38. Glossary

casa de cambio	An exchange house used to bring foreign currency into the country
Castellano	The Spanish language as it is called in Argentina
CDI *(Clave de Identificación)*	Argentinean tax ID, similar to social security number in the US
cell phone	Known as a mobile phone in the UK and Europe
certificado de domicilio	A proof of address certificate issued by the police
citizenship	The status of being a citizen of a country with full rights and duties and being eligible to apply for a passport
civic liability	Legal liability to other parties in respect of accidents. Similar to third-party liability in the UK
condominium	A purpose-built apartment block
corporation	Alternative name for a company or business
corporation tax	Annual tax on a company's profit
counteroffer	An offer made in return by one who rejects an unsatisfactory offer
departamento (dep)	Spanish for apartment
departamentos	Administrative areas (departments) within a province
DNI *(Documento Nacional de Identidad)*	A small government-issued booklet that contains information about someone's identity including a number that uniquely identifies them
double taxation treaty	Tax treaty between nations that ensures tax is only paid once where laws and jurisdiction of the countries overlap

The Complete Guide To Real Estate Investment In Argentina

Downtown	The heart of the city center
Edificio	A building such as an apartment or office block
Elevator	Known as a lift in the UK
Escribano	A lawyer qualified to deal with property transactions who is also a *notario publico*
Escritura	The act of taking possession of a property formalized by an escribano
Expensas	A monthly bill sent to owners of residential units detailing the running costs of the building
Flete	Delivery - e.g. of furniture
forex costs	Bank charges for converting between currencies
Garante	A guarantor a landlord can pursue if a tenant doesn't pay the rent
Garantía	A guarantee given by a garante to cover the tenant's rent in the event of non-payment (used for long-term rentals)
Garbage	Known as rubbish in the UK
Gazumping	Losing out on a property deal because someone else offers a higher price before the deal is legally binding
Gran Buenos Aires	Greater Buenos Aires - the area of the city beyond the boundaries of the Capital Federal
hot tub	Known as a bath tub in the UK
Impuesto al Valor Agregado (IVA)	VAT - Value Added Tax (sales tax in US)
Inheritance	At the owner's death property passes to the heirs or those entitled to succeed

38. Glossary

Inmobiliaria	Spanish for realtor (estate agent in UK)
inmuebles	Spanish for real estate (property)
Inspección General de Justicia (IGJ)	Public body with responsibilities for company creation and registration
inventory	A formal list of the items contained within a rented property
La Boca	A colorful, rough working-class barrio with potential to be rejuvenated
landlord's withholding tax	21% of the rent paid
lien	The legal claim of one person upon the property of another person to secure the payment of a debt or the satisfaction of an obligation
lobby	Same as entrance hall in the UK
long-term rental	Rental period of 2 years or more
luminosity scale	A number between 1-10 that measures the amount of natural sunlight an apartment receives
master agency	Where one agent is responsible for managing a property (the master), but other agents may also provide tenants
Microcentro	Downtown - the very heart of Buenos Aires and the business center
municipality	A city, town, or other district possessing corporate existence and its own local government
notario publico	A notary public - someone legally empowered to witness signatures and certify the validity of documents
notarize	To certify a document or cause it to become certified through a notary public

The Complete Guide To Real Estate Investment In Argentina

occupancy rate	The percentage of the total time available that a property is rented
pago adelantado	Payment in advance
Palermo	The largest barrio, subdivided into smaller districts
Parquet	Floor composed of short strips or blocks of wood forming a pattern. Very common in Argentina
Peso	Argentina's currency, denoted by $
planta baja (PB)	Ground or street level floor inside a building (first floor in US)
Plastificado	Lamination of a new parquet floor with lacquer (a kind of varnish)
Porteria	Caretaker or concierge
power of attorney	Written authorization to act on someone else's behalf in a legal or business matter
property management	When a rental agency is responsible for organising repairs and general maintenance. Can include payment of bills etc. on behalf of the landlord
property specification sheet	Describes the specification of a property for sale, may include photos or a floor plan
property title	A formal document that serves as evidence of ownership and describes the property
Puerto Madero	The old port area, now being rejuvenated
Rapi Pago	A chain of stores where people can pay their utility & other bills
real estate investment consultant	Provides advice on the real estate market to clients and assists with purchasing and refurbishment

38. Glossary

realtor	An agent appointed to sell property (estate agent in the UK)
Recoleta	Buenos Aires' most exclusive barrio
remis	A private-hire taxi that is pre-booked
remodelar	Spanish for refurbishment
reserva	The reservation fee you have to put down when you make an offer to prove you are serious
residency	Having official authority to live and/or work in a country in accordance with the terms of an issued visa. Can be temporary or permanent
Retiro	Upscale barrio adjacent to Recoleta
return on investment (ROI)	The ratio of money gained (or lost) on an investment in relation to the amount of money invested
rubrication	To be officially stamped in red ink
San Telmo	The oldest barrio, renown for its antiques fair and shops & the birthplace of tango
security deposit	A sum paid by tenants to be used against any damage they may cause
seguro	Spanish for insurance
sena	A private contract between the buyer and seller that works in a similar way to a boleto
serviced apartment	Rented to short-term guests where amenities for daily use are provided
short-term rental	Rental period of less than 6 months
sole agency	Where only one agency is used exclusively

The Complete Guide To Real Estate Investment In Argentina

stamp tax	A tax levied by the national and/or provincial governments that is a percentage of the sale price
Stock	Known as shares in the UK
Subte	Buenos Aires' underground (metro) system
transfer tax	Tax payable on selling a property equal to 1.5% of the price
trash can	Known as a rubbish bin in the UK
Upscale	At the upper end of a social or economic scale
VAT	Value added tax (similar to sales tax in US)
Warrant	A form of authorisation to another party
Yield	Another term for return on investment

39. Supplementary Appendix Information

This book gives you all the hard facts you need to know about real estate investment in Argentina. It tells you *what* you need to know.

What the book does not do is to recommend specific individuals or businesses - e.g. consultants, realtors, lawyers, escribanos, tradesmen and rental agents etc. that are known to be trustworthy, ethical and reliable - in short the very people you should be doing business with so that you can invest in Argentinean real estate with complete confidence that you are not being exploited or ripped off. The author provides this information in the form of a supplementary appendix which can be downloaded from his website for a charge.

The supplementary appendix is updated regularly and contains specific information about recommended businesses and individuals in relation to all areas of this book. It also covers any relevant changes that have occurred since the book was written and includes the latest news on real estate prices and trends.

Taken together, the book and the supplementary appendix provide a complete guide not just to *what* you need to know, but also crucially to *who* you need to know to successfully invest in Argentinean real estate.

Details about purchasing the supplementary appendix can be found at: **www.simon-a-fawkes.info**

Notes

www.ingramcontent.com/pod-product-compliance
Lightning Source LLC
Chambersburg PA
CBHW032009170526
45157CB00002B/614